Centering the Margins

Perspectives on

Literatures in English

from India, Africa, Australia

This publication has been generously assisted by the Australian Academy of the Humanities.

Centering the Margins

Perspectives on
Literatures in English
from India, Africa, Australia

CYNTHIA VANDEN DRIESEN

PRESTIGE

Published by
Prestige Books
New Delhi 110 008

1995

ISBN: 81-85218-99-4

Photo Typesetting by
Pivot Computers
Delhi 110 006
Ph. 2934490

Printed at
Mehra Offset Press
New Delhi 110 002

for

IAN

Contents

Acknowledgements

I wish to acknowledge the use of materials previously published in the following books and journals.

"Swami and Friends: Chronicle of an Indian Boyhood," in *R K Narayan, Critical Perspectives*, ed. A L McLeod, Sterling, New Delhi, 1994.

"Patterns in the African and Indian Post-Colonial Experience. Narayan and Achebe," in *South Asian Responses to Chinua Achebe*, ed. Bernth Lindfors and Bala Kothandaraman, Prestige, New Delhi, 1993.

"Slave-girls and Career-girls—Representations of the West African (Ibo) Female—Emecheta and Achebe," *SPAN,* Special Issue, Vol. II, No 36, October 1993.

"Jung the Artist and Patrick White," *St Marks Review* (Canberra) No 119, September 1984. Reprinted in *Australian Literature Today* ed. R.K. Dhawan and David Kerr, New Delhi, Indian Society for Commonwealth Studies, 1993.

"The Holy Fool in the Novels of Patrick White" in *Patrick White, Life and Writings*, ed. Martin Gray, Centre for Commonwealth Studies, University of Sterling, Scotland.

"'Devils, . . . Savages' and 'Nobler Forms.' Post-Colonial Reinventions of the Indigene in Works by Patrick White." Conference Proceedings, University of Barcelona, Sitges, Spain. October 1993. (In the Press)

"Interview with R.K. Narayan"—versions of this interview have appeared in *The Indian Ocean Review*, Vol V, No 3, 1992, and *SPAN* October 1992/May 1993, Vol II, Nos 34 and 35 (Double Issue).

"Kindling Australian Studies in Korea," *Australian Studies* No 17, April 1990.

I have to thank Dr. R.K. Dhawan, Secretary of the Indian Society of Commonwealth Studies (ISCS), for his interest in securing the publication of this work.

I am grateful to Edith Cowan University for its generous sponsorship of international conference attendance and its interest, at the highest levels, in promoting the research interests of its academic staff.

I must acknowledge Rosemary Seneviratne's dedicated labours in getting this manuscript ready for publication before a highly-pressured deadline.

The interest and support of my family—at all times—is appreciated, unendingly.

Preface

The essays in *Centering the Margins* were originally written as articles for journals, chapters in books or papers for conferences. Most of them have developed from my research and teaching interests over the past six or seven years. Only two of the essays included here ('Swami and Friends . . .' and 'The Artist and Society . . .') can trace their genesis to earlier phases of my research. They are included here because, despite the recent frenetic changes in theoretical approaches to literary works, they retain an intrinsic interest and indeed have recently been selected for reprinting elsewhere.

The thinking represented here reflects, in a sense, aspects of that 'decolonizing of the mind' that is a necessary part of the intellectual progress of someone like myself, the product of a colonial education system.[1] Born and educated first in Sri Lanka my literary preferences were originally shaped by the study of the canonical works of the British literary tradition. 'Discovery' of the scope and richness of the 'new' literatures was essentially a postgraduate adventure of exploration from which I have never looked back. This broadening of intellectual horizons has coincided with life experiences that have permitted first-hand observation of, and immersion in, the varied geographic and socio-cultural contexts from which these works derive.

Part of the ongoing intellectual adventure has also been the relinquishing of older modes of literary analysis as their inadequacy to uncover the ideological subtleties of literary texts became apparent. Foucault's teachings have demonstrated how older beliefs regarding the universally given are discursive ideological constructs relevant to a specific historic time and situation.[2] Readers of post-colonial texts particularly need to be aware of how their own consciousness is historically constructed and the relevance of their own identity has to be counted in their encounters with these texts.

Whatever the shortcomings now being identified in Said's classic work *Orientalism*, his investigations (derived from Foucault's notions of discourse) have shown the interrelationships between text, knowledge and power, how Orientalism defines its own norms and concepts relating to the Orient and prescribes its own exclusions.[3] If Foucauldian theory has shown that 'truth' is only what counts as true within a prescribed system of rules for a particular discourse and power is that which annexes determines and verifies truth, the 'truth' of any representation is determined by the possessors of power—in the discourse of colonialist texts—by the colonial regime.

Postcolonial critics are concerned to interrogate and undermine hegemonic structures and to explore the possibilities—however constricted these may be—of creating alternative versions of truth. If

Orientalist 'truths' have been created by speaking from within eurocentric perspectives only, their interrogation must acknowledge the need of speaking from a different cultural perspective—no less than from within that othered landscape, the terrain of the Orient itself. Besides this space for speaking from a different cultural perspective there must also be space for experiences with other texts situated as far as possible from the mesmerizing dominance of the Centre. This is where the discourse between the margins needs to come into play as a mode of displacing the continuing cultural hegemony of the Centre. Admittedly these propositions have their problematic aspect. They involve a form of resistance to Western ideology based on Western intellectual perspectives. This resistance need not be the less authentic however and the possibility of genuinely interventionist criticism need not be precluded because of this hybridity in the critical position. Postcolonial texts themselves partake of this condition of hybridity.[4]

Said's insistence (in turn borrowed from Gramschi) on the importance of compiling one's own 'inventory of traces' is a necessary first step in negotiating the post-colonized terrain. In compiling my own (and acknowledging Althusserian ideas of the interpellated subject) I believe I would have much in common with the third type of interpellated reader (of the three models defined by Pêcheux); the reader aware of the discursive forms working on her and seeking to deliberately exploit these so as to work against these hegemonic forms, a process Pêcheux labels 'disidentification.'[5] Awareness of the power of dominant ideologies confers the possibility of their transformability.

Postcolonial critics working towards dismantling colonialism's signifying system need, not only to identify literary devices that have deprived the colonized of voice but also, to explore the possibilities of assisting the restoration of those suppressed voices, to re-voice the silence. In the critics' anxiety to tease out the theoretical subtleties pertaining to this discourse and its imbrications in a range of disciplines—sociology, history, politics, there is a need to avoid marginalizing the texts themselves—*the* medium through which the once-suppressed voices find expression. Even if the myth of the single unified consciousness (of the author in the text) has now been permanently displaced the different cultural perspectives of the multiplicity of textual voices need to be acknowledged. This is where the challenge in reading and responding to, as well as in teaching and critiquing these 'new' literatures now resides.

Articulation of this need for theoretical discussions to be ballasted with an awareness of the specificities of the various cultures from which these texts derive need not attract the charge of essentialism. The 'new' reading position demanded of critics concerned to subvert Orientalist discourses on the Orient requires acknowledgment not only of the interpellated nature of their own subjectivity but also of the interpellatedness of the voices in the texts they choose to explore. The growing gulf between the theorists and the producers of the texts imbricated in their discussions needs to be negotiated.[6] Attending to the cultural specificities of the varied constituencies from which these texts are generated would appear a necessary safeguard against the tendency to construct these heterogeneous groups as monolithic categories, which is simply to continue the practices of Orientalism.[7]

Part of the project for reclaiming the cultural terrain must also involve some re-direction of critical energies into exploring the nature and sources of demotic cultural resistance in indigenous cultures which have enabled them to survive—albeit in a changed or hybridized form—the deleterious onslaughts of colonialism. Continuing to focus on the nuances of the discourse of the Imperial Centre and the ex-colonized margins is a mode of perpetuating the cultural hegemony of the former. Of the three writers—from different regions—whose works are dealt with in this collection of essays, each has envisaged his own cultural group as forming his primary audience and each has affirmed in one way or another a belief in his people's capacity for self-regeneration.[8] The ex-Empire does not appear so much concerned to write back to the Centre, as to write back to itself, and thereby to write *itself*. Exploring the discourse of margin with margin—new patterns of intertextuality—may be productive of surprising insights; could in fact, rather than homogenizing these constituencies emphasize their heterogeneity.

Postcolonial theorizing, as Benita Parry in her insightful review of current discourse indicates, needs to proceed beyond the continuing preoccupation with the binary of colonial Self/colonized Other, of Centre/Margin.[9] While the exploration of the varied modes of the silencing effects of colonization will continue for a while yet there is also a need to explore the forms of resistance which have subsisted. Preoccupation only with the interaction of colonizer and colonized contributes to a form of neo-colonization. While acknowledging the contribution of some of the most influential interventionist voices in the field—Spivak, Bhabha, Jan-Mohammed, Parry identifies what she still perceives as a falling short of the real needs in the project for re-claiming the once-colonized terrain for the post-colonized. She cites rather the practice of Frantz Fanon and his dialogical interrogation of European power and native rebellion as writing a text that could answer colonialism back. Fanon conceded that while transitional forms would for a while show a degree of assimilation of the occupying power's culture, this would, in time, give way to a 'literature of combat,' addressed to 'a new public' and delineating new horizons for the national consciousness. Parry believes that

> Fanon's theory projects a development inseparable from a community's engagement in combative social action during which

> a native contest initially enunciated in the invader's language culminates in a rejection of imperialism's signifying system. This is a move which colonial discourse theory has not taken on board and for such a process to be investigated, a cartography of imperialist ideology more extensive than its address in the colonialist space as well as a conception of the native as historical subject and agent of oppositional discourse is needed. (Parry, 1987, p. 45)

While Spivak protests the obliteration of the native's subject position in imperialist texts, she also writes out evidence of native agency, by passing, it would seem, the evidence of the years of India's struggle against British dominance; while Bhabha elucidates the native's stratagems for undermining the British colonialist text, he does not look to decipher an alternative text or recognize its possibility.

Parry acknowledges the significant differences in the critical practices of Bhabha and Spivak but feels that they are both

> submerged in a shared programme marked by the exorbitation of discourse and a related incuriosity about the enabling socio-economic and political institutions and other forms of social praxis. Furthermore, because their theses admit of no point outside of discourse from which opposition can be engendered, their project is to place incendiary devices within dominant structures of representation and not to confront these with another knowledge. (Parry, 1987, p. 42)

Taking stock of current intellectual positions recently, Said himself was moved to state that the idea that the impact with the West was "the main thing that counts in the history of these (excolonized) societies" is now problematic:

> . . . the new generation of historians is looking at that impact as simply another episode among many in a much longer history than that provided by 'the impact of the West.'

In his discussion he indicates the inevitable limitations of investigations which remain shaped only by the dominant Western traditions such as the neglect to explore the nature of Islam apart from the threat it presented to Western security. In the same episode, another discussant amongst the panelists mentions a conference where the all-Asian participants had met to discuss "Endogenous Elements in Native Cultures" and where all of those present appeared to be mostly preoccupied with "the West, the West, the West"; the Japanese participants, who alone did not speak in English, discussed the topic solely in Japanese terms, "they never referred to the West at all." What could be prefigured here is the real possibility that with the increasing economic ascendancy of Asian powers (Japan, China, Korea, Indonesia, Malaysia) the cultural hegemony of Europe will itself be challenged in new ways.[10]

Critical approaches in this wide field need to be eclectic. In my own critical practice, I have found that exploitation of the expanding dialogue between language and literature studies have been productive and capable of transmutation over a range of cultural contexts. Strategies in colonialist texts (identified by Said) as modes of constructing the non-European Other can be used to highlight similar structures operating in reverse mode in post-colonial texts. Spivak's identification of the historically-silenced native as the subaltern woman can be set against Chandra Mohanty's affirmation of the possibilities of locating women's voices in the post-colonial text.[11] Texts need to be opened up to admit a plurality of readings. Bakhtinian concepts of the polyphonic text as well as Machereyan strategies for deciphering the unconscious of a text (distinct from the personal unconscious of the writer) afford a range of useful strategies for investigating the multi-faceted potential of the post-colonial text. In this collection of essays, critical practices have ranged freely through these possibilities.

In the end, perhaps the most that attempts to create a counter-hegemonic discourse will achieve will be only an uncovering of

> small and relative and provisional truth one that eschews the naivety of any supposedly direct access to reality . . .[12]

In a post-modern climate which will not, in any case, admit the possibility of any grand récit, the circulation of such 'small' truths can still be productive by reason of their interventionist and transformative nature.

This collection of essays concludes with an Appendix which considers some of the challenges attendant on the push to globalize interest in these so-called 'new' literatures in countries like Japan, Korea and China where they are still relatively unknown. In such regions their attraction stems from the possibilities they offer of interrogating the Eurocentric biases of hegemonic English literatures (British, American) *as* the literatures of the 'margins.' The time is surely come for 'centering the margins.'

NOTES

1. Ngugi Wa Thiong'O, *Decolonizing the Mind* (London: Heinemann, 1986).
2. See Paul Rabinow, 'Truth and Power' (from Power/Knowledge) in *The Foucault Reader* (New York: Penguin, 1984), pp. 51-57.
3. Aijaz Ahmad's are perhaps the most recent strictures which have drawn the limelight:

> Said's procedures are radically anti-Foucauldian and are taken directly from the high Humanist traditions of Comparative Literature and philology which have shaped his narrative method and his choice of texts . . .

See Aijaz Ahmad '*Orientalism* and After: Ambivalence and Metropolitan Location in the work of Edward Said' in *In Theory: Classes, Nations, Literatures* (London: New York: Verso, 1992), p. 167.

Some of Ahmad's objections could be answered by invoking Pêcheux' idea of the subject constructed through the process of 'disidentification,' described above (See Note 5) Said's cautionary procedure of compiling his 'inventory of traces' also has a relevance here.

4. See Bill Ashcroft, Gareth Griffiths and Helen Tiffin, *The Empire Writes Back* (London: Routledge, 1989), p. 180.
5. Michel Pêcheux—using Althusser's ideas on how ideology 'interpellates' (constructs) individuals as subjects—describes three modes in which subjects may be constructed: 'identification'—those who freely accept their discursive formation; 'counter-identification'—a total rejection of the offered image; and 'disidentification';—those who combine an awareness of the forces within them with a determination to work against those forces. Pêcheux posits his reasoning on post-Freudian (Lacanian) teaching of the primacy of language in the construction of subjectivity.
   See Ch. 9, 'The Subject-Form of Discourse,' in Michel Pêcheux, *Language, Semantics and Ideology,* trans. Harbans Nagpal (London: Macmillan, 1982).
6. Several recent Conferences—such as the SPACLALS Conference (Fremantle, 1992) and the recent 'New Cartographies: Commonwealth and Post-Colonial Literatures Conference' held at Oxford University (April 1995) saw the surfacing of this divergence at the Conference forums.
7. This is a trap into which some western feminists have fallen, the construction of the women of the third world as a monolithic category.
8. Patrick White hoped his writing would create in Australia "a race possessed of understanding," 'The Prodigal Son,' *Australian Letters*, 1, 3, 1958, p. 40. Achebe hoped to help his people "to look back and try and find out where we went wrong, where the rain began to beat on us," *Morning Yet on Creation Day* (London: Heinemann, 1975), p. 44.
   Narayan declared 'I can't write a novel without Krishna, Ganesha, Hanuman, astrologers, pundits, temples and devadasis or temple prostitutes . . . that has turned out to be my India . . ." See Ved Mehta 'Profiles: The Train Had Just Arrived at Malgudi Station,' *The New Yorker*, Vol. 6, No. 1, 1962, p. 54.
9. Benita Parry, 'Problems in Current Theories of Colonial Discourse,' *Oxford Literary Review,* Vol. 9, Nos. 1 and 2, 1987.
10. See 'The Intellectual in the Post-Colonial World' (Response and Discussion held at Skidmore College on April 10, 1985) in *Salmagundi*, 70, 1, (Spring/Summer, 1986), pp. 70-71.
11. See Chandra Mohanty, 'Under Western Eyes: Feminist Scholarship and Colonial Discourses,' *Feminist Review*, 30, August 1988, pp. 61-88.
12. Peter Hulme, *Colonial Encounters* (London: Methuen, 1986), p. 7.

1

R.K. Narayan's *Swami and Friends*: Chronicle of an Indian Boyhood[1]

Graham Greene, Narayan's earliest Western admirer, wrote enthusiastically of *Swami and Friends:*[1]

> [it] brought India . . . in a sense of the Indian population and the Indian way of life, alive to me. . . . Swami's is the story of a child written with complete objectivity, with a humour strange to our fiction, closer to Tchekhov than to any English writer with the same underlying sense of beauty and sadness.[2]

Generally, the appeal of this early novel appears to have remained somewhat unappreciated. Its autobiographical element is one aspect of interest. Despite the fact that it is now some years since literary theorists have been bidden to take note of the death of the author, there is still considerable evidence to suggest the continued accordance of a privileged position to the writer. Foucault explains this as a continuing mode of privileging certain writings over others and expresses a hope for the eventual development of 'a form of fiction which would not be limited by the figure of the author.' In the meantime he admits, 'It would be pure romanticism were I to imagine a culture in which the fictive world operates in an absolutely free state . . . still, as our society changes, . . . the author function will disappear.'[3] That time, it seems, is yet to come.

Moreover, in that type of fiction in which an autobiographical element is particularly strong, it is precisely the persistence of the authorial shadow that imparts a special piquancy to such writings as D.H. Lawrence's *Sons and Lovers* or James Joyce's *Portrait of the Artist as a Young Man. Swami and Friends*, in Narayan's own words, grew out of 'the urchin days at Ammanis,' the boyhood days spent in his grandmother's home.[4] According to L.D. Rubin, however, even without such external evidence, the impression would be conveyed by 'the way the story is written, by the kind of details, by the value placed on certain events, very unimportant events often, which nevertheless are obviously being remembered and recaptured.'[5] The impression may be registered through a fleeting glimpse (as, for example, of Swami daydreaming in his classroom, contemplating the unattractive physiognomy of his class-master or hopelessly yearning for a hoop), or a more detailed elaboration of incidents, such as the clash with the Scripture-master or the joys and disappointments of cricket. Throughout, there is the elusive but unmistakable impression that 'out of the confusion of his past experience the writer creates order and acceptance.' (*Rubin*, 397)

As a novel of boyhood, this work has little of the strong dramatic interest deriving from a plot replete with adventurous exploit and unusual incident such as characterises a novel like *Huckleberry Finn*. Geared though it is to the relatively unexciting routine of everyday life and the petty drudgeries of school, an unobtrusive but marked pattern slowly emerges. Swami is himself too young and lacking in self-awareness to evaluate his experience, but the narrative voice (perhaps the adult looking back on past experience) subtly marks a progress. An apparently casual sentence records early: 'This was Swami's first shock in life. . .' (31). Subsequent episodes present a series of such shocks, which operate as factors in the boy's emotional development. Swami is not explicitly presented as consciously learning from experience, but he does progress. For example, early in his novel he almost confides his fear of the coachman's son to his father, but he 'suddenly decided that his father had better not know anything about the coachman's son, however serious the situation might be' (92). Instead, he arms himself with a sharp stone. After his second clash with the school authorities, he runs away and has wild visions of being sent to Trichinopoly or Madras to work and earn but finally accepts that, "After all, I shall have to go back to the Board High School. . ." (73).

The early episode of Swami's clash with the Scripture-master highlights the innate impulsiveness that appears to be at the root of his troubles. Rajam is driven to remark, 'What a boy you are, always in some trouble or other wherever you go, always, always. . .' (147). His troubles, however, plumb a deeper depth than the kind that a William (of the tales by Richmal Crompton) endures.[6] Swami's experiences are intimately bound up with his schoolboy friendships—particularly his hero-worship of the boy Rajam. The novel begins with a series of minor incidents, each working to its own crisis and resolution. Swami's next predicament, the clash between his attraction to Rajam and his loyalty to Mani, is again quickly and happily resolved. The third incident is really the first of the more important crises, educative in their influence. Swami is deeply confused by the inexplicable hostility of his erstwhile cronies: 'His cheeks grew hot. He wanted to cry. . . . Not a word reached

Swami's brain, in which there was only dull pain and vacuity' (31). A moment like this indicates a dimension of feeling impossible for Richmal Crompton's William. Yet, with typical boyish resilience, he is soon diverted, watching a piece of tin float down the gutter. Later he even grows 'accustomed to his position as the enemy of Somu and company' (33). This action is not followed directly to its conclusion. A variation in the tempo gives a sense of variety and also establishes a sense of the continuing passage of time. In fact, though the narrative time covers only a period of one year, the impression is of a complete tract of experience, an entire phase of life, as it were. Rajam's visit to Swami's home and the attendant preparations (apart from enforcing a sense of their deepening friendship) conveys the sense of the currents of ordinary life going on around the central dramatic events. Episodes such as the arrival of his baby brother, his chats with Granny, or the occasional domestic exchanges between his parents have the effect of rooting the central figure of Swami in a concretely authenticated domestic context.

After exams and the excitement of the holidays, a second significant episode, probing a deeper level of experience, is enacted. The coachman's son's duping of Swami involves him in deeper horrors: 'He had in his heart a great dread of the boy, and sometimes in the night would float before him a face dark, dirty and cruel, which made him shiver. It was the face of the coachman's son.' (75) Even the physical surroundings into which he blunders as a result are unnerving: 'urchins with their prodigious bellies, women of dark aspect . . . scurvy chickens, mongrels. . .' (76). Nowhere is the impression of the minutiae of the routines of everyday life flowing smoothly around the active, experiencing mind of the young boy better conveyed than in the subsequent chapter: Swami enjoys his holiday pranks, suffers acutely from his father's attempts to teach him arithmetic. Father's conciliatory gesture of taking him to the club brings him, all unexpectedly, face to face with the coachman's boy again and an evening of abject terror ensures.

The next significant episode is Swami's involvement in the nationalist agitation. The outcome of events now grows darker. Swami is expelled from the Albert Mission School. The brief narration of changes (Swami in his new school and the dispersal of his set in the old) conveys the impression of a lapse of time before the final and most important episode. The animated scenes of the founding of the Cricket Club, the problems of equipment, and the trials of practice build up the sense of the tremendous importance of the match in the eyes of the boys. Interwoven with these are the details of ordinary life, such as the incident of Granny and her lemon. Swami's attempts at compromise between the intransigent demands of the Board school discipline and his own intense desire to fulfil the expectations of his friends reaches a crisis in his clash with the Board school headmaster. His running away provokes the major crisis of the lost match and the estrangement from Rajam, which is, for Swami, the ultimate tragedy. His misfortunes have mostly been the very direct result of the operation of Swami's own qualities of character and temperament on circumstance. It is only at the very last—in Rajam's going away—that there is the suggestion of the intervention of an inscrutable fate. Moreover, it is Swami's own procrastination in seeking a reconciliation with Rajam that prevents him from learning of it earlier and thus materially lessening the shock. Swami is here confronted with an impersonal situation that makes his own regrets or Rajam's forgiveness seem finally irrelevant. It is a fitting culmination to the widening cycle of experience to which he has been subjected. The physical travail of his experience on the Memphi Forest Road now appears to be complemented by an emotional breakdown. Acceptance appears impossible. At the station he raves at Mani, and his cry, 'Oh Rajam, Rajam . . . when will you come back?' (178) shows his increasing loss of self-control. Finally, he breaks down and sobs. It is the kind of behaviour impossible to Crompton's William, but then William is purely a figure of comedy; Swami seems more nearly a figure drawn from life.

Each of the shocks that Swami experiences has the effect of being underlined through the fact that in each instance physical suffering in some form accompanies the mental experience. In the clash with Somu and Co., there is a hand-to-hand fight; in the episode of the coachman, Swami is stoned; in the nationalist struggle, he is assaulted by the policeman. An ascending scale of severity appears to be depicted until in the last episode he is found unconscious by the carter and it is only 'after hours of effort with food and medicine that the boy was revived' (164). Yet there is no effect of unrelieved pessimism. Some crises (even the episode of his running away) work out to fortunate conclusions: Swami enjoys the companionship of his friends, Granny's indulgence and also his parents' affection, though he himself is less aware of this fact.

The effects of comedy also help preserve a sense of detachment, so that Swami's trials are rendered in perspective. Often it is through the presentation of the exaggerated working of Swami's over-active imagination that the comic effect is created, such as in his imaginative involvement with Rama and Krishna, which prevents his working out a problem in arithmetic. At the same time, this exaggeration functions as a comment, a pointer to his boyish inexperience, impulsiveness, and irresponsibility. Even at the height of crisis, a comic note is struck:

'Swami shuddered as he realised what a deep-dyed villain Dr Kesavan was . . . he would not allow that villain to feel his pulse even if he [Swami] should be dying of fever!' (144) Exaggeration, in fact, appears to be the favoured device for comic effects, as in the description of Ebenezer's Scripture class: 'Tears rolled down Ebenezer's cheeks when he pictured Jesus. . . . Next moment his face became purple with rage' (5); or in the characterisation of Mani: 'He came to the class, monopolised the last bench, and slept bravely. No teacher ever tried to prod him. It was said that a new teacher who tried it very nearly lost his life' (8). There are also the comic effects that spring from incongruities of situation, such as Swami's reflections on his class master's unattractive appearance while the latter corrects his homework, or the Board schoolmaster found asleep. Inextricably twined with the comedy are the touches of pathos, as in Swami's desperate attempts to scrape together a few annas for a hoop: he even tries magic. Often the pathos derives from the complete indifference of the adults (except, perhaps, Granny, herself a marginalised figure) to his keenest wants.

The final scenes of Swami's parting from Rajam are remarkably serious in tone, underlining the effect of a particularly painful and climactic experience. One has the impression that Swami's feelings are kept under control simply because he is obliged to keep at a distance from his friend physically because of the crush at the station. When he does face him briefly, 'Swaminathan lost control of himself' (178), but before emotion can really gain the upper hand, Rajam is whisked away. The scene is quite remarkable for its technique: the mechanics of the action ensure that feeling is kept within bounds, although the poignancy of Swami's situation derives from his state of complete emotional breakdown. The narrative voice maintains a fine balance between humorous detachment and empathy with the central figure.[7] It is apart from and yet involved in the experience of the central character, who is only dimly aware of the full implication of events. The reader is aware of a gap between the level of awareness of the naive protagonist, the boy Swami, and the more inclusive consciousness of the narrative voice. In the autobiographical work this voice acquires the inflections of the authorial personality looking back on past experience. The movement between these levels of consciousness is skilfully effected. In the depiction of Swami's involvement with the nationalists, for instance, in such a statement as "He paused and said on the inspiration of the moment 'We are slaves of slaves' . . ." (93), it is the authorial voice speaking; but soon after, the focalization is Swami's: 'The persons who cut off Dacca muslin . . .' (105). Frequently, the narratorial voice gives way imperceptibly to Swami's own perceptions: 'The back of his head and pink ears were visible to Swami. . . . Swami was in intolerable suspense that the head should turn and fix its eyes on his . . . If only somebody would put a blackboard between his eyes and those pink ears.' (105)

Swami's consciousness of the inimical quality of the adult world, his aversion to the rigours and discipline of school or study, his hero-worship, his impulsive enthusiasms and yearnings (whether for the possession of a hoop or the joys of cricket and the companionship of kindred spirits) refract the perennial experiences of boyhood. His dilemmas recall the predicaments of Pip, of David Copperfield, of Huckleberry Finn—fictive characters whose joys and frustrations still affect readers across time and space. Yet Swami (like them) remains, finally, a creature of a particular time and place. He belongs, recognisably, to his Indian environment. When hungry his longings are for ghee and curds; when he is lost; his terrors are of elephants, yellow and black tigers, cobras, scorpions, demons. In his fear, 'he prayed to all the gods that he knew. . . . He promised them offerings . . . to roll bare-bodied in the dust, and take alms to the Lord Tirupati' (160). On a subtler level, the rough, pioneering, independent spirit of Huckleberry Finn is as foreign to him as the sophisticated concern with social graces that occupies the young boy of Tolstoy's *Childhood, Boyhood and Youth.* Swami emerges as a very ordinary and undistinguished boy, and perhaps this ordinariness enhances his representative quality. He is attracted to the Pea because of the similarity of disposition: 'he was just ordinary, no outstanding virtue of muscle or intellect. He was as bad in arithmetic as Swami was, he was apprehensive, weak and nervous . . . the bond between them was laughter' (9). Part of the sense of a 'rounded' portraiture (in the Forsterian sense) derives from the enfolding circle of domestic relationships and routine within which Swami is placed, pictured upsetting his mother by grabbing the baby's cloth, alternately bullying or humouring his granny, adroitly avoiding his father's eye, or ignoring his mother's admonitions. His peculiar mixture of timidity and boldness renders his actions continually capable of surprising—and yet, in retrospect, completely credible.

The minor figures emerge with similar clarity, mostly in terms of their impact on Swami. It is his visual impression and attitude that colours the presentation of 'Fire-eyed Vedanayagam' or the Board school headmaster: 'The wizened, spectacled man was a repulsive creature with his screeching voice' (172). Swami's particular friends, Mani and Rajam, are developed in greater detail than the others in this band. Mani is largely a figure of comedy (the element of exaggeration in this portraiture has been noted earlier), with his great brawn and little brain. His depths of loyalty and devotion render him a veritable tower of strength to Swami for whom he acts as spokesman and agent in moments of crisis. Even as the insignificant David is attracted to the glamorous Steerforth in *David Copperfield*, Swami is dazzled by the mental and physical accomplishments of Rajam. Rajam's material possessions—his car, his clothes, his toys, and even his father's position—further establish him as a superior being in Swami's eyes. Unlike Steerforth, Rajam appears wholly deserving of respect. His physical and mental superiority is repeatedly dramatised in such episodes as his deliberate challenge and later equally deliberate placation of Mani, his pacification of the faction of Somu and Co., and his calm confrontation of the Board school headmaster. His style of speech dramatises this poise. When Swami makes his excited complaint against the coachman, 'He has duped me of two annas . . .,' Rajam interposes, 'My dear boy, twelve pice make one anna and you have paid thrice six pice each time; that is eighteen pice in all,' and on Swami's protest insists, 'But in money matters you must be precise' (74). The contrast of character is dramatically enforced.

Even in this earliest novel of Narayan's the English language functions wholly credibly as a medium of expression for Indian characters. In the conversation of the schoolboys, their quick animosities and changing enthusiasms, their joys and their disappointments are conveyed with a sense of authenticity and immediacy:

> 'Are you a man. . . . Which dog doubts it? Have you the courage to prove that you are a man?' 'How?' . . . 'Meet me at the river' . . . 'What for?' 'To see if you can break my head' . . . 'Oh, to pieces!' (17)

The novel appears to have little overt concern with political and social issues. The illusion of the boy's world is consistently preserved; the political riots do not appear more significant to him than his clash with the coachman's urchin or his loss of Rajam. Yet the reader is also made aware of the concrete impact of the larger events of India's colonial history on these individual lives. External details such as street names (Lawley Extension, Grove Street) or peripheral events presented (such as the nationalist unrest) are reminders that the setting is an India under British rule. There are more subtle details. Part of the admiration accorded Rajam is for his European clothes; 'socks and shoes, fur cap and tie and a wonderful coat and knickers' besides his ability to speak English 'exactly like an European' (45). Swami and his friends are fanatical cricketers. Swami's father plays tennis at the club. Nevertheless, the emerging nationalist pride in *khaddar* (homespun) clothing is symptomatic of new forces at work. Swami's schoolboy world can be directly affected by larger political and social issues; his participation in the nationalist demonstration makes him feel guilty towards Rajam, whose father is a deputy superintendent of police, owing loyalty to the British Government. Earlier, the Pea makes only a gesture of disapproval of the Scripture-master's conduct; being a Christian, he basically approves the master's criticism of Hinduism. Swami's reaction is much more nationalistic in its resentment.

There is in the Malgudi of this early novel a definite quality of the idyllic reflected, for example, in the descriptions of the River Sarayu, which bounds it on one side, 'glistening like a silver belt across the north' (13). Its other boundary is 'the thick belt of Memphi Forests' (157). The suggestion of isolation further enhances this idyllic quality, emphasised also by the constant evocation of the intimate connection with the rural village. Thus, country carts lumber along the Trunk Road and herds of cattle ford the stream at Nalappa's Grove. Swami's route along the Trunk Road is 'shaded by trees bearing fruits, the white ball-like wood-apple, green figs and deep purple eugenia peeped out of thick green foliage' (158).

The autobiographical novel, unlike the autobiography, is not to be tested by its fidelity to biographical fact. Paradoxically, its peculiar advantage over the biography is that often by its very departure from literal fact it is able to show the whole truth of a character or situation, the deeper logic or pattern of meaning that ordinary life itself might obscure. Thus Henry James, though he often took a character or incident from life as a starting point for a novel, deliberately refused to follow the rest of the facts, in which he saw only 'clumsy life at her stupid work.' In his discussion of James Joyce's *Portrait of the Artist as a Young Man* and D.H. Lawrence's *Sons and Lovers,* Pascal shows how the departures from biographical fact are dictated by the overriding authorial intention of giving a special pattern to events, impressing a motif which works finally towards evoking a more general and representative significance from events described.[8]

Narayan's own departures from ascertainable biographical fact work in the same direction. For example, although much of the material derives from the period of his life which he spent with his grandmother in her own home, a much indulged grandson, he presents her here as a singularly powerless and pathetic figure. Thus the young boy's essential defencelessness against the generally indifferent and inimical adult world is emphasised. Again, where the boy Narayan was one of a *large* family comprising five brothers and two sisters, Swami of the story has one brother—and that a baby. The logic behind the change is self-evident: the focus is completely on Swami; his conflicts and predicaments are highlighted in a manner impossible to achieve were he made to share the stage with a host of sibling figures.

NOTES

1. Page references are to the Indian Thought Publications edition of *Swami and Friends*, Mysore, 1971.
2. Graham Greene, Introduction to R.K. Narayan's *The Bachelor of Arts* (Mysore: Indian Thought Publications, 1970), p. vii.
3. Michel Foucault, 'What is an Author?' *Literary Criticism and Theory*, ed. Robert Con Davis and Laurie Finke (New York: Longmans, 1991), pp. 729-35.
4. Ved Mehta, 'Profiles: The Train Had Just Arrived at Malgudi Station,' *New Yorker*, Vol. XXXVIII (15 Sept. 1962), p. 55.
5. L.D. Rubin. 'The Self Re-captured,' *Kenyon Review*, Vol. 25, No. 3 (Summer1963), pp. 391-99.
6. One critic reads it as "a gentle more charming, South Indian version of the British Richmal Crompton's 'William' books'," see Williams, H. Moore, 'English Writing in Free India 1946-1967,' in *Twentieth Century Literature*, Vol. 16, No. 1 (Jan. 1970), pp. 1- 12.
7. This provides an interesting adaptation of two of the three fundamental narrative situations identified by Franz Stanzel as 'authorial' and 'figural.' In the former, the narrative proceeds from a point of view external to the action; in the latter, the point of view remains with one of the actors. The third category is the first-person narrative situation. See Franz Stanzel, *Narrative Situations in the Novel* (Bloomington: Indiana UP, 1971). These relatively simple schema admit of a remarkable degree of elaboration, as shown by Gerard Genette, *Narrative Discourse* (Oxford: Blackwell, 1980).
8. See L. Pascal 'The Autobiographical Novel and the Autobiography,' *Essays in Criticism*, Vol. 9 (1959), pp. 141-45.

2

Parallels and Pointers: Patterns in the African and Indian Postcolonial Experience

> Our discipline is now spending so much time critiquing colonialist discourse that the genuinely new directions implicit in the study of the new literatures in English are being neglected. Deconstructing imperialism keeps us within imperialism's orbit.[1]

Diana Brydon's suggestion that we need to attend to the variety of writers' voices speaking from different positions within the field and to start with these rather than Derrida, Lacan or Todorov as a means of "reconfiguring our sense of the possibilities and dilemma of our enterprise" appears to be a timely one. It could be that theoretical debates have dissipated energies so that interesting lines of comparison between the works of literary artists drawn from widely different cultures yet linked by the cataclysmic experience of colonialism and their common use of the English language (or an "english") have not been explored.[2] Comparative studies in the field are sparse considering the period over which it has now engaged critical attention.[3]

As Said has indicated (and Brydon herself notes) one's own position in relation to the field is of some significance.[4] Compiling my own "inventory of traces" would involve a recognition of the mixture of influences in my background which would tend to produce a kind of hybrid. Now an Australian citizen, I am of Sri Lankan origin and the product of a Western-oriented educational system and life experiences which have involved teaching and studying for extended periods in Asia, Africa and Australia. Years ago the Indian novelist and critic Balachandra Rajan suggested that "the man with mixed allegiances is contemporary Everyman".[5] The post-colonial literatures particularly offer the possibilities of exploring this idea; of highlighting striking similarities and significant differences between the experiences of the hybrid products which are the inevitable result of the clash of cultures subsumed under the term colonialism. These are emphases which should not be disregarded if we are re-discover through the discourse on those literatures, those "humanistic values" which Said has shown that Orientalism "by its scope, experiences and structures, has all but eliminated".[6]

Some of these writers, perhaps because of the consistency of their preoccupations and the substance of their achievement, have acquired a recognizable role almost as chroniclers of their people's experience. Chinua Achebe indeed saw his work as affording Nigerians the opportunity "to look back and try and find out where we went wrong, where the rain began to beat us".[7] India's R.K. Narayan in a career spanning over five decades has produced a group of novels that provide striking insights into a crucial phase of Indian experience. Comparison of a work by each of these writers clearly set in the postcolonial era promotes an awareness of striking similarities as well as some aspects of remarkable difference. They reflect in some measure, through the dilemmas of the central characters, attempts of these societies to readjust, as it were, after the shock of the colonial experience, a shock which for these traditional societies was also synonymous with the beginnings of their advent into the modern technological age.

Despite their widely different cultural contexts there is an essential kinship of experience and outlook between Achebe's Odili in *A Man of the People* and Narayan's Raju in *The Guide*.[8] Odili seems to be a later mutation of Obi Okonkwo of *No Longer at Ease*, more amoral, more detached from the claims of family, tribe or religion. Raju, more strikingly than other Narayan protagonists, appears similarly liberated from restrictions of traditional beliefs and observances. For both, self-interest appears the only guide to conduct. Odili's involvement in politics grows simply out of his desire to be revenged on Chief Nanga for the humiliation over his girlfriend, as earlier his moral objections to the politician dissolve easily at his invitation to the city and the prospect of an easy scholarship. Raju has no compunction in posing as a holy man since it ensures an easy livelihood at the expense of the poor villagers, as earlier he commits forgery to ensure continuance of his luxurious lifestyle through the exploitation of the woman he supposedly loves. In fact both these antiheroes acquire the distinct aspect of parasites. Odili seems less adept than Chief Nanga at exploiting others at the start, but by the end of this deeply pessimistic novel he has learnt from the master, so that party funds will be diverted to pay his bride-price for Edna without a qualm on his part.

For both young men the ties of family, of religion, of tradition are meaningless. If the mother-figure in traditionally oriented societies is presented as the repository of tradition, it is interesting to note the representation of this figure in these novels. Obi Okonkwo's mother (in

Achebe's earlier novel) is an ailing old woman but her significance as spokesperson for the traditional order is underlined when she remonstrates with her son on his decision to marry an outcaste woman. Later Obi experiences a sense of relief at her death. Significantly in this later novel, Odili's mother has died in childbirth and he is taunted as the "bad child that crunched his mother's skull" (*MP*, 32). His father is also identified with the alien power, having been a District Interpreter under the British regime.

Raju's position in relation to the mother-figure appears only marginally different. She is compelled to leave the house when he insists that Rosie lives with them and the rout of tradition appears complete. Yet unlike in Achebe's work, this rout is later shown to be only temporary. One recalls then that Raju's mother has remained as a central figure in the household for several years and the grown man Raju is deeply moved:

> "I had seen her for years at the same time sitting with closed eyes . . . it now filled me with sadness that I should not see her there any more (*G*, 155).

To continue, for the moment, to trace the broad parallels between these young men, each reveals even in his pursuit of his romantic interests, the same amoral self-interest, even a kind of calculated callousness that undercuts any suggestion of idealism or romance. Neither is deterred by the fact that the woman he is attracted to is legally or morally committed to another man: her husband in Rosie's case, her fiancé in Edna's. Traditional taboos are equally meaningless. So Raju is unaffected by the fact that Rosie comes from the caste of temple dancers, while Odili is unconcerned that Chief Nanga has already paid the bride-price for Edna. Both adopt a calculated, deliberate kind of strategy, trying out particular tactics and detachedly assessing their success even with the women they supposedly love. Having decided that he would "go back, seek out Nanga's parlour-wife, and give her the works, good and proper" (*MP*, 86), Odili observes the effect of his early moves: "She was not in the least surprised by my offer. She was obviously the trusting type which augured well" (*MP*, 105). Raju assesses his progress in the seduction of Rosie with similar calculation: "I praised her dancing. I spoke out my love but sandwiched it conveniently between my appreciations of her art. . . . It worked" (*G*, 74). While he seems to experience some degree of genuine attraction to his mistress this seems subordinated at will to his own self-love. Raju suppresses information about her husband from Rosie and commits forgery rather than risk his luxurious lifestyle; Odili unleashes a stream of calculated insults in a letter as the only possible revenge when he thinks he is losing Edna.

Within each novel the writer presents a sketch of the more traditional woman besides which the portrait of the "new" woman who engrosses the young man's attention must also be measured. In both, remarkably, the traditional figure appears appreciative of the "new" woman's achievements. Mrs Nanga accepts philosophically (except for one outburst) the idea of her being too unfashionable and insufficiently educated and refers to Edna as "our" wife. The criteria for the selection of the "parlour-wife" are education and good looks. Yet even Odili registers a sense of the vitality and strength of Mrs Nanga. Her abuse of him after his betrayal of Chief Nanga leaves him more shaken than the encounter with Nanga himself. Edna actually appears naive in comparison to Mrs Nanga and seems far more dominated by the male figures in her experience.

In fact women, despite their careers as lawyers or nurses in the new society, still seem tied to subordinate roles as sex objects to the men they encounter. Even the "most sophisticated-looking young woman" introduced to Odili as "Barrister Mrs Akilo" provokes the following reaction:

> I must confess to a certain awkwardness before her sophisticated, assured manner. The way she spoke she must have spent her childhood in England. But this awkward feeling was only momentary. After all, I told myself, Chief Nanga who was barely literate was probably going to sleep with her that night (*MP*, 53).

Yet it is one of these new, young, educated women who is also recorded as making the only significant gesture of protest against the general deterioration of the nation's moral and political life. Reflecting on Max's fiancé's avenging of his death, even Odili concludes that

> Max was avenged not by the people's collective will but one solitary woman who loved him. . . . For I do honestly believe that in the fat-dripping, gummy eat-and-let-eat regime just ended . . . you died a good death if your life had inspired someone to come forward and shoot your murderer in the chest without asking to be paid (*MP*, 167).

The world reflected, particularly with regard to the status of women is very much a world in transition in both novels. In the venal city, Odili competes with Nanga for the favours of amenable females. While at one stage apparently discounting the traditional observances with regard to the formal procedures of marriage when he wishes to persuade Edna she has no obligation to marry Nanga, he later exploits these practices when it seems they would serve his purpose. He formally establishes his own claims to Edna through paying the traditional bride-price but shows again the cynical amoral consciousness of the new generation in his cool decision to use party funds for this purpose:

> I had already decided privately to borrow the money from CPC funds still in my hands. They were not likely to be needed soon (*MP*, 165).

A similar medley of figures fills the background of Raju's life in Narayan's novel. The traditional figure of the mother waiting obediently on her husband's pleasure and abiding by the advice of older male relatives or faithfully serving the household gods, is drawn with considerable sympathy. Like Mrs Nanga, the traditional female figure in Achebe's novel Raju's mother, one notes, is not without an appreciation of the value of education and its potential. She is thoroughly approving of Rosie's having gained a Master's degree in Economics, declaring "You are not like us uneducated women. You will get on anywhere" (*G*, 126).

The peculiar mixture of tradition and modernity that characterizes both novels, especially in their portrayal of the roles of women and marriage and match-making in their different societies, is particularly apparent in the case of Rosie. As an intellectual Marco had shown himself sufficiently uncaring of traditional taboos to marry a woman belonging to the caste of temple dancer, and Rosie's possession of a Master's degree offsets the traditional disqualification. After marriage he appears to treat her as something less than human as she comes a poor second to his complete absorption in his work. Raju cunningly establishes his hold upon her through exploiting her genuine passion for her own art and through promising to further her career as a dancer. Later after his unprincipled exploits lead him into the Law-Courts he recognizes that Rosie possesses enough resilience to continue without his help. More convincingly perhaps than in Achebe's novel, Narayan projects a sense of the potential of the new woman. Economic independence appears to be the key factor as Raju realizes:

> I was now a sort of hanger-on in the house; ever since she had released me from police-custody, the mastery passed to her (*G*, 195).

The existence of an older way of life alongside the growing manifestations of the new adds piquancy to the settings of these novels. One encounters that curious amalgam of lingering tradition and invading modernity that can perhaps only be appreciated fully by those who have had some direct experience of living in these cultures. It is finally this context of living that provides the background for the development of the new hybrid anti-hero and must therefore in some way provide a part-explanation of why and how he is what he is.

In Achebe's novel the opening sentence immediately focuses on the significant conjunction:

> No one can deny that Chief the Honourable M.A. Nanga M.P., was the most approachable politician in the country (*MP*, 1).

The juxtaposition of the tribal title alongside the Western honorific of the imported British political system sets the keynote for the way of life subsequently portrayed in the novel. The previous section has already highlighted the blur of confused situations relating to women and to marriage. It is no exaggeration to note that this mixture of elements is present in all the facets of life presented—food, clothing, housing and the whole range of social and personal relationships and interactions.

Odili's father regales himself with a "jar of palm-wine every morning and a bottle of schnapps now and again" (*MP*, 35). In his "peace offering" to his father, Odili is obliged to include "a bottle of schnapps, two bottles of White Horse and a bottle of Martell" (*MP*, 35). Apparently unconscious of any irony Chief Nanga rejects Chief Koko's offer of tea or coffee as drinks for "black white-men" and suggests "whisky and soda for me and Mr Samalu" (*MP*, 37). Since this is the era after independence, Chief Nanga is splendidly garbed in traditional robes. He takes the young writer Jalio to task for his unconventional dress: "Either you wear a suit . . . or if you don't like it you can wear our national costume" (*MP*, 70).

Ensconced in the comfort of his suite in the Minister's home Odili reflects:

> The surprises and contrasts in our great country were simply inexhaustible. Here was I in our capital city, reading about pails of excrement from the cosy comfort of a princely seven bathroom mansion with its seven gleaming, silent action, water closets (*MP*, 46).

Social events reveal the same mixture of influences. Christmas is celebrated with a presentation by masked dancers. The degeneration of the tribal past is perhaps most poignantly presented here when the rope ostensibly restraining the Mask comes undone:

> One might have expected this sudden access to freedom to be followed by a wild rampage and loss of life and property. But the Mask tamely put his matchet down, helped his disciples retie the rope, picked up his weapon again and resumed his dance (*MP*, 109).

The ultimate status symbol in the new society is, of course, the motor car. Odili's father despises his son's meanly paid occupation:

> He would . . . tell me [Odili] for the hundredth time to leave 'this foolish teaching' and look for a decent job in the government and buy myself a car (*MP*, 35).

Odili observes the fact that "In our country a long American car driven by a white-uniformed chauffeur and flying a ministerial flag could pass through the eye of a needle" (*MP*, 65). The Americans have indeed arrived on the Nigerian scene. Achebe's portrayal of the American presence—their desire to befriend, to please the "locals" and (perhaps, unwittingly) to patronise them is etched with a light but pointed satire.

Narayan's novels, written over a period of fifty years, reflect subtly the variety of changing features in the Indian scene. In *The Guide* the changes over the years are quite remarkably telescoped into the one novel. From the idyllic country scenes of Raju's boyhood, Malgudi develops rapidly into a busy town where tourists arrive daily by train on the newly built railway. Shops, theatres, photographic studios develop apace. Modernity and tradition co-exist visibly and the relics of the Raj are now sights for the tourist along with archaeological artefacts of interest to scholars. In the closing scenes of the novel the American arrives (the new colonizer?) with his television camera placating, seemingly considerate, but ultimately exploitative. Raju, now the holy man, reacts with traditional dignity where the younger Raju's reaction one feels would more nearly have resembled Odili's mixed feelings of attraction and hostility as he felt himself obscurely challenged by this latest mutation of the colonial power and the forces of modernization.

Raju's father had acquired a horse and carriage which had made him "the talk of the town" (*G*, 34) but throughout the main events Gaffur's taxi features most significantly and the trains whose coming had only been foreshadowed at the beginning thunder through Malgudi bringing more visitors, more business, more complications in their wake. His father's house had been built by his own hands:

> He had dug the earth, kneaded the mud with water and roofed them with coconut thatch. He planted papaya trees around . . . a single fruit brought him eight annas if carved with dexterity (*G*, 10).

Raju at the height of his career enjoys a lifestyle suited to a modern entrepreneur of the first rank:

> The stylish house at New Extension was more in keeping with our status. It was two-storied, with a large compound, lawns, garden, and garage . . . I had a large staff of servants a driver . . . two gardeners . . . a Gurkha sentry . . . and two cooks . . . (*G*, 166)

Raju revels in being able to serve his guests whiskey in a land of prohibition. Like his Nigerian counterparts he recognizes this as a mark of status. Throughout his varied career Raju's dress consistently presents that eccentric combination of East and West that seems so characteristic of his world. As tourist guide he wears a Khaki bush-coat and *dhoti* he sports "rimless glasses—(a present from Marco)" and a wristwatch (*G*, 157).

In postcolonial India there is also the sense of a resurgence of indigenous art. Rosie begins her meteoric rise to fame with Raju's successful persuasion of the local school Committee to set aside "the usual Shakespeare tragedy" in favour of an Indian dance recital at their annual social. One of those minor points of contrast between Raju and Odili is the former's positive feeling for his country's art. He appears genuinely moved by the aesthetic appeal of Nalini's performance:

> It [the snake-dance] was her masterpiece. Every inch of her body from toe to head rippled and vibrated to the rhythm of the song which lifted [her] into a creature of grace and divinity and an ornament of the gods . . . I was captivated by it (*G*, 184).

Achebe's satirical sketch of the Minister of Culture presiding at the function of the Writers' Society, humiliating the young Jalio by comments on his unorthodox dress and carelessly displaying his ignorance of the country's best-known writer requires little comment. Odili's behaviour is not more edifying. He feels himself humiliated when young

Jalio shows he has no recollection of their earlier acquaintance and is simply distracted for the rest of the time:

> I didn't listen much to Chief Nanga's speech. When Elsie and I were not whispering into each other's ears I was thinking about the night or even about such irrelevant things as the dress of some of the people in the room . . . (*MP*, 71-72)

In both texts, their use of a first-person narrator ensures that the language itself refracts and directs an insight into the central character. In Achebe's novel, in which the first-person narrator is used consistently, the effect is particularly marked. Narayan's pure and limpid style has been frequently commented on by the critics. This derives partly from the relative sparsity of untranslated words (though a few of these e.g. *dhoti, pyol* occur) and the lack of a significant attempt to superimpose local dialectal rhythms or syntactical structures upon standard English in the manner of most post-colonial writers endeavouring to evoke the sense of a specific cultural location.

With the recurrent flashbacks, the novel is so structured that we hear the recognizable tones of Raju recounting his past adventures, his cynical humour pervades all of these sections. The language acquires a marked colloquial flavour as when he expresses his annoyance at Marco:

> What does he take me for, this fellow, telling me that he wanted the car at this hour or at that hour--did he think I was a tout? It made me very angry, but the fact was that I really was a tout, having no better business than hanging around. . . (*G*, 61).

The shallow cynicism militates against any suggestion of a depth of feeling. Note his account of the growing estrangement between himself and Rosie:

> We were going through a set of mechanical actions day in and day out . . . fussy organizers . . . the same middle sofa in the first row . . . congratulations and off to catch the train—pocketing the most important thing—the cheque (*G*, 172).

The neutrality of the authorial voice when it takes over achieves an unobtrusive (and necessary) distancing of Raju's consciousness as the complex forces of spiritual regeneration begin to work in him. The final presentation of Raju the saint immolating himself for his people is presented from the viewpoint of the all-knowing narrator and maintains a sense of final ambivalence.

The language in Achebe's novel works consistently as a mode of self-revelation. Achebe's use of Odili as narrator means the tones of this morally and emotionally dehydrated anti-hero recur throughout. Arthur Ravenscroft describes him as "self-accused" in the rotten society of *A Man of the People*, primarily through his own language: "the words themselves reveal a shallow personality".[9] Note the flat pedestrian description of the events of the evening leading to his break-up with Nanga:

> I retired soon after dinner so that the others might take the cue. And Elsie did. The second time I peeped out she was no longer there in the sitting-room. But Chief Nanga sat on stolidly looking at the file of the speech he had already given. Every two minutes or so I came to the door and peeped out. . . (*MP*, 77).

His reaction to his betrayal can only be conveyed in clichés, "I was transfixed to the spot. . . . What went on in my mind at that time lacked form and I cannot now set it down. . ." (*MP*, 77). The ending is simply bathetic:

> I did not think anything particularly. I just bit my lower lip until it was sore. Occasionally words like 'Good Heavens' escaped me and came out aloud . . . 'My word!' I remember saying. . . (MP, 79).

The language itself establishes the personality as shallow and emotionally impoverished.

Usually, the occurrence of pidgin in the postcolonial text indicates a form of communication between classes, of ruler and ruled (in the earlier context of British rule) or later between the privileged, educated and the uneducated and unprivileged. Nanga and Chief Koko speak to their cooks in this manner. Yet often the use of pidgin between social equals, as here, suggests a special collusion in wrongdoing, a kind of deliberate mutually agreed on refusal to recognize codes of correct behaviour. So Chief Nanga addresses his brother politician Chief Koko in pidgin even as he swaps stories of his amorous conquests with Odili in the same medium.

In Achebe's earlier novels the introduction of Igbo proverbs into the language works towards incorporating a sense of native rhythms and syntactic structures, creating thereby a sense of the cultural distinctiveness of the context. In those novels which recreate the Igbo past it is an important means of establishing a sense of the wisdom and richness of that past. In the "modern" novels there is a hollowness of effect. Gareth Griffiths has shown how they underline a sense of the growing inadequacy of the proverbial language to function in a world whose values are framed in directly opposed terms.[10] So the proverb relating to the punishment of the man who took so much that the owner noticed had relevance in the traditional context where some amount of wealth is recognizably communal but as Odili realizes "in the affairs of the nation there was no owner, the laws of the village became powerless" (*MP*, 167).

If the city is synonymous with the technological modern civilization of the West, the village remains in every culture the last stronghold of the traditional communal life. In its simplest terms Raju's spiritual regeneration is secured by his actual physical removal from the corrupting influences of the town to the relatively unspoiled life of the village. The simple faith and piety of the villagers are the prime factors in transforming the ex-convict into the saint.[11] Raju rediscovers in the village the integrated existence which fell apart in the life of the towns as a result of the contact with the West. Daily the villagers worship at the feet of the "holy man" and absorb his words in the shrine by the river. Raju himself recognizes that the strength of this humble piety in Velan is itself the ultimate threat to him:

> Every respectful word that this man employed pierced Raju like a shaft. "He will not leave me alone," Raju thought with resignation, "This man will finish me . . . (*G*, 209)

Achebe's novel portrays no such survival of a reservoir of traditional pieties. The new values of materialism and individual self-interest have invaded the village as well. The village of Ananta is solidly behind the corrupt Nanga and (a direct reversal of the pattern of events in Narayan's novel), Odili's first acquaintance with the wily politician takes place in the village. When he abandons his job as village teacher to sample the opportunities of the big city, his moral destruction is ensured. Apparently the Minister sends his children to the village periodically. As Mrs Nanga explains, "Without it . . . they would become English people" (*MP*, 43). Other details show however that the city values have invaded the village. Take the instance of the returning students:

> We call them holiday makers and their presence has a way of immediately raising the general tone of the village, giving it an air of well-dressed sophistication. The boys I saw that morning wore

> Italian-type shoes and tight trousers and the girls wore lipstick and hair stretched with hot iron. . . (*MP*, 107).

It is in this survival of the village and particularly of the religious traditions within it that the postcolonial scene as portrayed in Narayan's novel contrasts with Achebe's portrayal of the Nigerian scene. In *No Longer at Ease* Achebe had already shown how lightly Christian religious beliefs sat upon the convert Nwoye's son Obi Okonkwo, *Arrow of God* had presented the traditional priest's recognition of what the coming of Christianity had portended. In the post-British era the Christian ethic appears as of little relevance as the traditional. Max's idealism (for which he is shot) has absolutely no relation to the fact of his being the son of a Christian missionary; he does not subscribe to his father's beliefs. Religion whether Christian or traditional is not a factor of any consideration to Odili. The only religious image of any significance emerges in the satirical lines of the last paragraph of the novel describing the corruptness of the era just past:

> a regime in which you saw a fellow cursed in the morning for stealing a blind man's stick and later in the evening saw him again mounting the altar of the new shrine in the presence of all the people to whisper into the ear of the chief celebrant. . . (*MP*, 167).

It is not that the new influences have not been felt on the Indian scene. The young Raju is impatient with the religious rituals so important to his parents but puts on a performance calculated to impress his watchful father:

> I washed myself at the well, smeared holy ash on my forehead, stood before the framed picture of gods . . . and recited all kinds of sacred verse in a loud, ringing tone. . . (*G*, 11).

Later as a young man about town he becomes involved with a young married woman who belongs to the taboo caste of temple dancers. His actions so scandalize his mother that she feels compelled to leave their home. Yet she has already ensured that some part of her own values have in fact been transmitted and will resurface at a later time. At the very moment of parting he recalls his memory of her praying daily before the household shrine and is so saddened that he would not see her there any more that he is moved to tears. Every night of his boyhood, waiting for his father, he had listened to her stories of Devaka ". . . a hero, saint, or something of the kind" (*G*, 19). Later on in his chequered career as he assumes the role of holy man he impresses his first disciple with "'Do you know the story?' He started narrating the story of Devaka. . ." (*G*, 17). The decision is explicitly made by his father not to send the boy to the local Albert Mission School because "it seems they try to convert our boys into Christians and are all the time insulting our gods" (*G*, 23).

If social changes and the corruption of the town have created the rogue, his removal to the village where the traditional pieties still remain appears to purge him of confusion. Narayan's protagonist ultimately shows a capacity for spiritual survival which seems related to the still lingering configuration of traditional forces. It could be held that Narayan's novel portrays a more optimistic vision of a society changed perhaps but not destroyed by the experiences of colonialism and modernization. Achebe's portrayal of a protagonist more nearly submerged in the rottenness of the "fat-dripping, gummy, eat-and-let-eat regime just ended" (*MP*, 167) appears more deeply pessimistic. Achebe achieves here in one sense his declared aim in writing, of helping his people "to look back and try and find out where we went wrong".[12] In any case in the wisdom and clarity of his portrayal, the poised detachment of his interpretation of facets of the experience of his people there is a continuing invitation to understanding and perhaps, cause for hope.

NOTES

1. Diana Brydon, 'New Approaches to the New Literatures in English,' *Westerly*, Vol. 34, No. 3, 1989, pp. 23-30.
2. Bill Ashcroft, Gareth Griffiths and Helen Tiffin, *The Empire Writes Back: Theory and Practice in Post-Colonial Literatures* (London: Routledge, 1989), pp. 38-77.
3. Arthur Ravenscroft, 'African Literature: Novels of Disillusion,' *Journal of Commonwealth Literature,* Vol. 6, 1969, pp. 120-37
4. Edward Said, *Orientalism* (New York: Random House, 1979), p. 25.
5. Balachandra Rajan, 'Identity and Nationality', *Commonwealth Literature: Union and Diversity in a Common Culture*, ed. John Press (London: Heinemann, 1965), pp. 106-9.
6. Said, p. 110.
7. Chinua Achebe, *Morning Yet on Creation Day* (London: Heinemann Educational Books, 1975), p. 44.
8. Page references in the text will be to the following editions: *A Man of the People* (London: Heinemann, 1966), abbrev. *MP; The Guide* (Mysore: Indian Thought Publications, 1975), abbrev. *G.*

9. Arthur Ravenscroft, pp. 122-23
10. Gareth Griffiths, 'Language and Action in the Novels of Chinua Achebe', *African Literature Today*, Vol. 5, 1971, p. 98.
11. Cynthia vanden Driesen, 'From Rogue to Redeemer,' R.K. Narayan's *The Guide*, *International Fiction Review*, Vol. 6, No. 2, 1979, pp. 166-70.
12. Achebe, p. 44.

3

Doughty Slave-Girls and Slavish Career Girls: Representations of the West-African (Ibo) Female in Selected Works of Emecheta and Achebe*

The slave-girl motif which first surfaces explicitly in Emecheta's novel with that title, is regarded as central to her work.[1] It should be read as a trope of defiance. Briefly, it tells of the passionate protest of a young slave-girl about to be ritually entombed with her mistress. Violently clubbed into an open grave, her cries continue to resound, till finally the earth smothers her. In Achebe's novel *No Longer at Ease*, the bawdy songs about "young women who had become nurses or teachers instead of mothers" (*NLE*, 2) implies a devaluation of female potential that appears to be refracted in other aspects of Achebe's works.[2] This paper will consider the contrasted representation of the West African female in the work of two writers, both Nigerian, both Ibos and both addressing (broadly) similar historical moments.

Bearing in mind the importance of the personal dimension as outlined by Said, compilation of my "inventory of traces"[3] requires mention of my life-experience of four years of living in Nigeria. The fact that my experience of West African women did not mesh with representations of them encountered in the works of male African novelists was one of the impulses behind this study. There is also a need to reiterate here a point made by Kate Millett. Granted that "literary criticism is not restricted to a dutiful round of adulation" investigations of the less flattering aspects of a work need not imply devaluation of the writer's achievement. It should be possible, for example, "to make a radical investigation which can demonstrate why Lawrence's analysis of a situation is inadequate, or biased . . . without ever needing to imply that he is less than a great and original artist, and in many respects a man of distinguished moral and intellectual integrity."[4] No devaluation of the work of Achebe is intended in the following study.

Chronologically beginning with Achebe seems appropriate. In these novels set in the tribal past, Achebe's narrative of the clash of tribal forces with the colonial oppressor is very much *his*tory. The shadowy female figures mutely fulfil their traditionally ordained roles as compliant wives, daughters and mothers. Okonkwo beats his wife for being late with his meal, even during a taboo period: "he was not the sort of man to stop beating somebody half-way through, not even for fear of a goddess."[5] His wives and daughters follow him in and out of exile having no individual destiny apart from their lord and master.

In *Arrow of God* where the claims and counter-claims of rival priests and elders, of the native people and the colonial power are so eloquently debated, the voices of women are conspicuously silent. The narrative focus might flicker briefly over bickering wives or a young bride at her wedding, but it is the fate of the dominant male which is foregrounded. When the chief priest is imprisoned by the colonial power, the only area of decision for the women has to do with which one of his wives should be sent to cook for him.

In works set in the contemporary world women may now be "nurses or teachers" but their roles seem even more circumscribed. Now, not even accorded the status of wives, they simply serve the sexual appetite of the male, whether fledgling bureaucrat or corrupt politician. Even a brilliant barrister must submit to the male narrator's salacious regard. In *A Man of the People*, Mrs Barrister Akielo, just arrived to meet the Minister, tells Odile, she hadn't even showered. His response:

> I thought she was beautiful even with the dust on . . . I felt momentarily awkward before her sophisticated, assured manner . . but this awkward feeling was only momentary as I told myself Chief Nanga who was barely literate would probably sleep with her that night.[6]

The American woman, the acquaintance of a few hours, must also simply succumb to African male virility. Not even a phone call in the midst of sexual intercourse can distract her:

> "Don't move . . . " commanded Jean . . . then with me and all on her she began to writhe on her back towards the phone . . . (*MP*, 52)

Later, she confides, "sex means much more to a woman than it does to a man." Achebe's modern females appear even more compliant than their traditional sisters.

Greimas' categories of the actants in a narrative (a development from Propp's work on the Russian folk-tale) can provide an invaluable insight into narrative structure.[7] These can help also to focus on those silences in the text which, in turn, provide clues to ideological stance.

None of the female figures in Achebe's novels function as "subjects" and/or "receivers." Neither do they fit any of the other functions of, "sender," "helper" or "opponent." At most, in *NLE* or *MP* they function partially as "objects", included as part of the male's goal of material success, signalled usually by the possession also of an attractive, educated wife. The marginalization of the female could not be more complete.

Before the appearance of Emecheta's first novel, *In the Ditch* (1972), Nigeria had passed through the traumatic experience of civil war (1967-1970). She herself was one of the students demonstrating in Trafalgar Square in London at the time.[8] Her earliest (strongly autobiographical) works recounting an African woman's struggle for survival with five children in London, won her early acclaim as one of those writers "who belie the myth that feminist issues are not important to African women."[9] Subsequent works interrogate the social and familial structures that regulated the life of the Ibo female into the earlier decades of this century. What Emecheta records is *her*story, the varying success of women seeking their own forms of self affirmation within the constrictions of the patriarchy. In *The Bride Price* (1976) Akunna successfully defies family and social taboos to marry her low caste lover.[10] Raw male aggression is subverted by female strategy when Okoboshi her kidnapper is frustrated of his lust. At the very moment he has forced her onto the bed and is untying his lappa,

> . . . she laughed like a mad woman . . . Look at you, she sneered . . . shame on you. Okoboshi. You say your father is a chief dog, chief that is what he is, if the best he can manage to steal for his son is a girl who has been taught what men taste like by a slave. . . (*BP*, 138).

This deliberate use of the image of the violated female body functions like a Medusa-head to terrify the male who is caught thus in his own male-created taboos. It is a motif that recurs also in *Destination Biafra* (1982). For the woman able to survive the ordeal, an important stage of her empowerment is reached.

Ojebeta in *The Slave Girl* (1977) shaves her head in order to escape the possibility of enforced marriage. She too, asserts her freedom in the choice of her marriage partner. Nnu Ego, in the ironically titled *Joys of Motherhood* (1988) could be regarded as the ultimate female victim of a patriarchal society which only valorizes her child-bearing capacity so as to perpetuate a society in which male privilege remains enshrined. Her capacity for survival, independent of the assistance of a token husband, establishes her as a symbol of female self-sufficiency.[11]

Greimas' categories of actants again provide a useful shorthand, permitting some conclusions as to the feminist ideology of these works. The "subject" and "receiver" functions are filled exclusively by female figures. Their "object" tends to be not so much a broad socio-political goal as with Achebe's male figures, but a more personally oriented goal of self-fulfilment. It is nevertheless an object which involves a breaching of social structures designed to ensure the continuance of male privilege. The function of "opponent" accrues consistently to the male figures, usually representatives of the patriarchal family. Emecheta does not oversimplify. Occasionally there is evidence of a degree of psychological collusion in her own disempowerment on the part of the protagonist herself. Besides there emerges also a degree of ambiguity in Emecheta's own authorial stance.[12]

Education functions most perceptibly as "helper." Often the degree to which defiance is sustained seems to be directly proportionate to the extent and quality of the education the protagonist receives. More significantly, these females each appears to possess, in varying degrees, a vitality, a quality of resilience that functions indubitably as helper. It seems also to function as "sender," the initiating impulse to defiance. I have designated this quality the 'Umuisagba' factor.[13] In *The Slave Girl* it is explicitly associated with the women from this particular village:

> This Umuisagba pride was so well known that some conservative homes were reluctant to marry girls from there . . . they never call the gods of their husbands' houses to help them—they would rather call on the goddess of the market to help them out. (*SG*, 11)

The protagonists occasionally show an awareness of some supra-personal factor, "a madness" or "a presence" that assists them in moments of crisis. Adah, in *Second Class Citizen* (1974), actually visualizes this Presence from childhood through to adulthood.

In Emecheta's *Destination Biafra* (1980) and Achebe's *Anthills of the Savannah* (1987), both works set against the backgrounds of political emergency, the two writers' representations of the West African female might seem to evince some surface similarity. In the text of *Anthills* Achebe seems to have inscribed in the words assigned the writer Ikem (an Achebe surrogate?) an apologia to women.[14]

In a somewhat arbitrarily introduced sequence, Ikem thanks Beatrice, the central female figure, for her gift to him of "insight":

> You told me . . . that my thoughts were unclear and reactionary on the role of modern woman in our society . . . you were right . . . a novelist must listen to his characters . . . (*AS*, 96)

Like Debbie, Emecheta's heroine, Beatrice seems to represent an attempt to explore the potential of the African female in a society reduced to a shambles by male decision-makers. Both women are represented as highly educated, ambitious, physically attractive, and socially so placed as to have access to the corridors of power. There the resemblances end.

Again, use of Greimas' model of actants can help highlight the divergences. The function of Emecheta's heroine Debbie as "subject"/"receiver" is clear; Beatrice's is more problematic. She shares the function with two other male figures, Ikem and Chris. As "helper" all three have education as well as intellectual and artistic gifts. Their "goal" appears to be the promotion of a political ideal of shared responsibility in which the privileged must reach out to the politically marginalized, the poor and uneducated. The "opponent" is identifiably the dictator with his ambitions.

In relation to the two male figures, the female is already marginalized since the narrative space accorded her is also circumscribed. Her function as subject begins to appear more superficial as the narrative progresses. Both male figures are accorded martyrs' deaths, Beatrice is scarcely bloodied by the action. Disappointingly, despite her superior advantages, Beatrice, like the career girls of Achebe's earlier works, seems to rely mostly on (what is vulgarly called) "bottom power" for survival.

She is first directly presented responding mutely to the peremptory summons of the dictator. Her resentment expressed in her refusal of the appropriate seat in the official car is, she recognizes, "a puny empty revolt, the rebellion of a mouse in a cage" (*AS*, 72). She is not permitted to accomplish more. At the dinner she fails in an apparently patriotic effort to supersede the American female for the President's attentions, and "her tears flowed in torrents" (*AS*, 81). For Beatrice male support seems indispensable to survival. First she leans on Ikem; next on Chris, and as soon as Chris is out of the picture, the Nigerian major provides a prop, with the young University student assisting for good measure.

Quite simply Beatrice spends too much time in bed with her lover to be convincing as a model for Nigeria's New Woman. When she does venture out to share part of Chris's last flight—the routine of a whole family is disrupted so Beatrice can be provided with a bed for her, by now, stereotyped contribution. An attempt to confer a "godessy" ambience on her remains too superficial.[15] She herself is allowed to claim, "I feel like Chielo" (*AS*, 114) but the only prophecy she articulates is a somewhat superfluous and belated warning to the already percipient men.[16] In their last encounter, Chris supposedly detects again this "godessy" ambience, but a goddess making despairing love in the discomfort of a bug-ridden bed in a one-room hovel is a strain on reader tolerance.

Serving the sexual appetite of the lordly male appears to be the limits of female destiny. Ikem Osodi, the sensitive writer, values Elewa more for her sexual athletics than her pure soul:

> . . . her love-making is just sensational . . . I suppose I shall never discover where in that little body of hers she finds the power to lift you up bodily on her trunk while she is curving upwards like a suspension bridge . . . And then—mixed metaphors—unmixed blessings, shake you like a miner panning for gold . . . (*AS*, 38)

Finished with, she is despatched home in a taxi at midnight; he would find it impossible to work with Elewa's hands "cradling his damp crotch" (*AS*, 38). That Chris should die in the attempt to protect a woman from the soldier's assault has a tinge of poetic justice. Shortly before, he and the young student have subjected the young woman to the characteristically (in Achebe's novels) predatory male scrutiny.

Where Beatrice's function in the Achebe work remains problematic, Debbie in Emecheta's novel, clearly and exclusively fills the role of "subject" and "receiver". Her "object" envisages unequivocally a self-fulfilment beyond the traditionally ordained roles:

> She wanted to do more than child-breeding and rearing and being a good passive wife to a man whose ego she must boost all her days. Yes she would join the army . . . It would be much more difficult for a woman . . . but she was going to fight. She was going to help . . . not as a cook or a nurse but as a true officer (*DB*, 45).

As "helper" Debbie has education and the social advantages that Beatrice has also been equipped with. Beyond this, she enjoys the energy of "the Umuisagba factor," as shown in her readiness to engage in a "more difficult" task, and her determination "to fight". As to be expected, her opponents, as with all Emecheta's heroines, are the male figures synonymous with the authority of the patriarchy, whose innermost bastions of privilege she attempts to breach in her choice of the army as a career.

In a war situation the sheer physical vulnerability of the female is exacerbated. As the Ibo soldier reminds Debbie's mother, devastated by the brutal rape of her daughter: "Give her water to wash herself. Hundreds of women have been raped so what? It's war. She's lucky even to be alive . . ." (*DB*, 135). Debbie suffers the ultimate act of male aggression when she is raped by the Nigerian soldiers. From being a biological hazard, her female body acquires through its degradation the Medusa-like power mentioned before. Debbie is able to taunt the Commanding Officer, who has also planned to rape her, secure in the knowledge he will not now touch her. The atrocities against woman are specifically slanted against her femaleness: the rape of the aged as well as of young women; the rape and murder of pregnant women and the slaughter of unborn infants. Women die in childbirth on the highways and newborn infants perish within days of birth. War becomes a theatre not for male heroics but for female endurance. Amongst Debbie's helpers are other courageous women: Mrs Madaka with whom she completes the nightmare journey to Biafra, her mother whose metamorphosis from social butterfly into gallant survivor inspires Debbie's own recovery.

The writer Ikem (Achebe's surrogate) admits to Beatrice, "I can't tell you what the new role for woman will be. *You* have to tell us . . ." (*DB*, 98), but a possible answer is suggested by Debbie in Emecheta's work. Beatrice at the end of Achebe's narrative is left still mourning her dead lover; Debbie is pictured on an airfield amidst a deadly rain of grenades and debris rejecting the chance of escape with her lover, her "male concubine" (*DB*, 259). In response to his question as to what she will do now she outlines her perception of the task ahead, in which the nurturant (female) role appears significantly conflated with the professional (male) role:

> There are two boys . . . and many other orphans that I am going to help bring up. . . . And there is my manuscript to publish (*DB*, 258).

* Selected Works by Chinua Achebe and Buchi Emecheta details of 1st publication, of editions referred to in this study, main characters and abbreviations of titles of novels

Chinua Achebe

Things Fall Apart. London: Heinemann 1958, 1987. Okonkwo. *TFA*.
No Longer at Ease. London: Heinemann 1960, 1964. Obi Okonkwo. *NLE.*
Arrow of God. London: Heinemann 1964. Ezeulu. *AG*.
A Man of the People. London: Heinemann 1966, 1976 Odile. *MP*.
Anthills of the Savannah. London: Heinemann 1987. Chris Oriko, Ikem Osodi, Beatrice. *AS*.

Buchi Emecheta

In the Ditch. London: Barrie & Jenkins 1972.
Second Class Citizen. London: Allison & Busby 1974. Adah. *SC*.
The Bride Price. New York: George Braziller 1976. Aku-nna. *BP*.
The Slave Girl. London: Allison & Busby 1977. Ojebeta. *SG*.
The Joys of Motherhood. London: Heinemann 1979. Nnu-Ego. *JM*.
Destination Biafra. London: Allison & Busby 1982. Debbie Ogedembgbe. *DB*.

NOTES

1. Katherine Frank, "The Death of *The Slave Girl*: African Womanhood in the Novels of Buchi Emecheta." *World Literature Written in English*, 21.3, p. 480.
2. Carole Boyce-Davies concludes that while 'Achebe's works are obvious classics within the African literary tradition, a re-examination of his work from a feminist position reveals woman as peripheral to the larger exploration of man's experience.' See "Motherhood in the works of male and female Igbo writers Achebe, Emecheta, Nwapa and Nzekwu" in *Ngambika*: *Studies of Women in African Literature* (New Jersey: Africa World Press 1986), 247.
3. Edward Said, *Orientalism* (London, Routledge & Kegan Paul, 1978), p. 25.
4. Kate Millett, *Sexual Politics* (London: Rupert Hart-Davis, 1971), p. xii.
5. *Things Fall Apart*, p. 21.
6. Achebe, *A Man of the People*, p. 52.
7. A.J. Greimas, *Structural Semantics: An Attempt at a Method*, trans. Daniele McDowell, Ronald Schliefer & Alan Velie (London: Univ of Nebraska

Press, 1983). See ch. x. "Reflections on Actantial Models," particularly pp. 207-9. In constructing a narrative grammar Greimas subordinates characters to action by calling them actants. He distinguishes between "acteurs" and "actants." The former can have specific qualities varying in different narratives the latter are general categories underlying all narratives. Both can include not only human beings but while acteurs are numerous Greimas' model has six actants only: sender—object—receiver—helper—subject—opponent.

8. Buchi Emecheta, Author's Foreword, *Destination Biafra*(London: Allison & Busby, 1982), p. vii.
9. Nancy Topping Bazin "Weight of Custom. Signs of Change: Feminism in the Literature of African Women," *World Literature Written in English*, 25.2, 1985:183-97.
10. Buchi Emecheta, *The Bride Price* (New York: Braziller, 1976).
11. "True feminism is an abnegation of male protection and a determination to be resourceful and self-reliant," Filomena Steady, *The Black Woman Cross-culturally* (Cambridge Mass: Schenkaran, 1981), pp. 7-36.
12. This ambiguity is explored in Rolf Solberg, "The Woman of Black Africa, Buchi Emecheta: The Woman's Voice in the New Nigerian Novel," *English Studies,* 3, 1983:247-61.
13. The Appendix to this paper indicates some of the factors subsumed under this term. All of these need more detailed exploration and analysis before an adequate feminist theory applicable to the West African context can be developed.
14. Achebe, *Anthills of the Savannah* (London: Heinemann, 1987).
15. The adjective appears to be Achebe's own coinage: "Chris had noticed . . . that she carried with her a strong aura of that other Beatrice whom he always described in fearful jest as 'godessy' . . ." (*AS*, 199).
16. In Achebe's novel *TFA*, the priestess Chielo is represented as a figure whose authority and power is respected even by the irascible Okonkwo (see ch.11, *TFA*).

Appendix

Some Distinctive Features of West African Women's Socio-Cultural Milieu

1. Conflation of motherhood with female identity: traditionally the female performed her tasks in the field or in the market-place with her baby strapped on her back, the roles of mother and worker were not dichotomous. (Emecheta dedicates *SC* to her children, "without whose sweet background noises, this book would not have been written". In *DB* Debbie's last speech envisages no conflict between the nurturant and professional woman's role.)

2. The polygynous household: This could provide a support system against the autocratic male. There was a degree of autonomy in the arrangement in the traditional context where each wife had her separate dwelling-place with responsibility for her own children. Economic factors made this a necessary arrangement. (*TFA*: the senior wife lies in order to protect a junior wife. *JM*: the two women conspire against their husband.)
3. "The 'Umuisagba' factor": This factor of the inherent vitality or resistant power of the West African woman is probably traceable to a number of factors in her traditional heritage. West African women have always enjoyed a degree of economic freedom and women regulated their own affairs in this sphere. The Ibo Women's War (1927), interestingly inscribed by colonial historians as "the Aba Riots", was an outcome of this independence of spirit. Through their trading and the marriage system, women actually had a wider "network" system than men. Women would also support each other in domestic difficulties. The custom of "sitting on a man" was one where women would come together to chant satirical songs and ridicule a man as a mode of containing male aggression.

The worship of goddesses, the power of priestesses, suggest other sources of female influence. Matrilineal ties were particularly important in times of misfortune. Colonialism destroyed this traditional world.

(The novels contain numerous instances of females supporting each other in times of familial or social stress. Even Okonkwo in *TFA* is compelled to show deference to the priestess, Chielo. His exile is spent in his mother's village. The Umuisagba factor is evident in such figures in Achebe's novels as Ezinma the daughter Okonkwo wishes had been a son, and in her mother who, despite being married to another man, walks into his hut to become his wife.)

* Most of the features mentioned as requiring investigation here necessitate exploration of historical, sociological and anthropological materials. Some useful works are: Sylvia Leith-Ross, *African Women*: A Study of the Ibo of Nigeria, London: Faber & Faber 1938 (an older, but still extremely informative study).

Ifi Amadiume, *African Matriarchal Foundations*: *The Igbo Case*, London: Karnak House, 1987. (The writer's thesis is that Igbo society is fundamentally matriarchal and has suffered an imposition of patriarchy upon it.)

Within parentheses are included broad references to supporting evidence in the texts of the novels referred to in this study.

4

Female Spaces in Male Narratives—Perspectives on Achebe and Narayan[1]

Frantz Fanon describes the colonial world as "a world cut in two . . . divided into compartments . . . inhabited by two different species . . ." The decisive factor in this compartmentalisation is the fact of belonging or not belonging to a given race . . . The cause is the consequence. You are rich because you are white, you are white because you are rich.[2] If the coloniser/colonised relationship is regarded as a paradigm of the male/female relationship of the patriarchy—this passage could also be read as follows:

> What parcels out the world is . . . the fact of belonging or not belonging to a given gender . . . you are powerful because you are male . . . you are male because you are powerful.[3]

It is because the nature of the physical space allocated the human being replicates the power structures of a society that the settler's town is 'brightly-lit', 'full of good things', while that of the colonised, is 'a world without out spaciousness . . . starved of bread, of light . . .'

The 'dividing line' which in the colonial city is marked by barracks and police stations is, in the gendered landscape of the patriarchy, more nearly the immuring door of the domestic dwelling. For western feminists it is the most recurrent site for the constriction of female potential; confinement within the domestic setting precludes woman's participation in those decision making processes that shape her world. One needs at this point to stress the need to attend to the cultural specificities of the texts to be explored. The continuing need is to interrogate any tendency towards constructing woman as a monolithic category. As Chandra Mohanty's important article has emphasised, there is a real need for Western feminist critics to take count of local cultural practices and socio-historical circumstances if they are to avoid the charge of ethnocentricism in their assumptions about women from other cultures.[4]

Attending to the cultural specificities involves a finer tuning in to the range of female constituencies. For Virginia Woolf possession of 'a room of her own' was, for the female artist especially, the essential condition for the articulation of her woman's voice. In the traditional Indian context, the secluded room was always available to the (middle-class) woman and while it ensured containment of female revolt, it was also simultaneously a recognition of its legitimacy.[5]

While it will be impossible to explore in any depth the status of woman in either the Indian or African contexts, within the time constraints of this paper, the range of possibilities will need to be briefly indicated.[6] For instance, in the Indian context the Laws of Manu encode the inferior and wholly dependent status of women, yet Hindu mythology is also replete with cultural imagery which portrays women as powerful and autonomous, rather than weak and dependent. The worship of the goddess Kali is important as an oppositional influence. A survival from the pre-Aryan past the goddess is an antagonist of all evil, but she is most significant as the embodiment of the female power principle. In Indian mythology, her annihilation of the mighty demon Raktabija by drinking his blood epitomises the destruction of the male principle. Her sexual dominance over Shiva further reinforces the figure of Kali as an enabling one for women. Regarded as a manifestation of Shakti, female divine power, this matriarchal myth is the central inspiration of the contemporary Indian Women's Movement.[7] It is no exaggeration to state that for some there is the expectation that the 'Kali Yuga' (Age of Kali) will see the destruction of the patriarchal universe and the restoration of an earlier matriarchal age.[8] These ambivalences in the Hindu tradition need to be borne in mind in exploring the implications of the positioning of the female figure in the Narayan texts. None of his works are placed, as Achebe's *Things Fall Apart* is, in a precolonial world, yet most of the female characters in Narayan's works adhere to traditionally accepted roles and values. There are some few who are also shown to be attracted to a more modern Westernised ethos, grasping after opportunities to break out of the traditionally ordained spaces and reach for the new possibilities being opened up primarily through India's encounter with the capitalist West. His earliest novel *The Dark Room* explores some of these tensions. The positioning of male and female, in the opening scenes, in terms of physical spaces, recalls the compartments of Fanon's description: the woman in her maternal role is fussing over a child. On her husband's entry she retires into the kitchen, meekly obeying his decree:

> Go and do any work you like in the kitchen but leave the training of a grown-up boy to me. It is none of woman's business. (*DR*, 5).

He passes into "the dining room," while she "hovered between the cook and her husband" waiting on him. Next, "he hurried away to his room and dressed for his office" (*DR*, 6). She is summoned to see him off at the door. Her economic dependence is underlined by the money handed her "to buy some vegetables." He strides out to the car, while she "lingered in the doorway" (*DR*, 7), the "dividing line" between her domestic and his public space. She still has one more duty within her allocated 'compartment':

> She went to the worshipping room, lit the wicks and the incense . . prostrated herself (*DR*, 7)

Her afternoon visits do not take her out of their street. She returns in time to "pick up the hoarse honking of the Chevrolet horn" (*DR*, 12) anxiously attuned to its nuances. Resentment against her husband's treatment of their son provokes a temporary withdrawal into the dark room. Kitchen, shrine room, dark room—within these spaces the traditional woman plays out her life. When Savitri actually leaves the home in despair because of her husband's infidelity, she finds work—in a temple. She returns because she misses "the comfort, security . . . of her home" and of course the children, "what a void they created." (*DR*, 123) Outside of her home she becomes the victim of other aggressors—even of the priest in the temple. Her friends, such as the irrepressible Gangu whose compliant husband preaches women's freedom, and Ponni the pickpocket's wife show the possibilities before the orthodox Hindu wife. The latter has the last word, approving Savitri's return home:

> . . . men are good creatures, but you must never give way to them. Be firm and they will behave. (*DR*, 125)

Most of the Narayan texts foreground a male consciousness. The females positioned in the interstices of the narrative abide in the traditional spaces allocated the woman within the Hindu household yet have an undeniable input into what is best described as the 'politics of the every day' as a glance at Margayya's wife in *The Financial Expert* will show. She is positioned most regularly in the kitchen, blowing up the kitchen fire, feeding husband and son, serving coffee to a visitor. His dramatic financial successes bring no change to her situation. The sense of the physical constraint of the domestic setting is even more suffocating because of the constant awareness of the brother's family beyond the partition wall, reacting to every event, shout or even smell in Margayya's household. She gives up her own small room, "eight foot square with no window" for his religious ritual at the start. Later, it is commandeered again for his money bags. Yet this most compliant of women is shown also to be endowed both with voice and agency over a range of situations. Her ridicule compels Margayya to wear the spectacles his vanity has prevented him from acquiring earlier. From her vantage-point in the home, "the mother watched the crisis developing" (117), the gradual estrangement between father and son. It is she who later propels the unwilling Margayya in search of his errant son and acceptance of the latter's disinclination for study and achievement. At the end, although his financial empire is in ruins, there is a sense of restored order:

> He relaxed completely. He lay on a mat his eyes closed, his wife is in the kitchen. . . (*FE*, 177)

Shortly after, "reaching for his grandson," he can still affirm, "I am going on with it" (*FE*, 128); his family, his home, "with the wife in the kitchen" at its centre have remained intact, the source of his resilience is clear.

In Achebe's *Things Fall Apart* again it is through exploration of the gaps and silences in the text that the reader becomes aware of female agency. Florence Stratton's view that it seems to be no part of Achebe's intention to restore dignity and self respect to African women requires some qualification.[9] Citing the first scene in which women appear—Nwakibie's summoning of his wives to share in Okonkwo's gift of palm-wine—Stratton sees their summoning and dismissal as evidence of their marginalisation. Yet the text itself is replete with details suggestive rather of woman's dignity and autonomy:

> Anasi was a middle-aged woman, *tall and strongly* built. There was *authority* in her bearing and she looked *every inch the ruler* of the women folk in a large and prosperous family. . . . She *walked up to her husband* and accepted the horn from him. . . . She rose, *called him by his name* and went back to *her hut* (15, *TFA*; italics mine).

The impression of women as an autonomous group with Anasi at their head is clear. There is no time here to expatiate on the variations between the S. Indian and W. African cultural contexts but I have cited elsewhere distinctive features in the Ibo woman's context which suggest a matriarchal substratum in the Ibo culture.[10] Here, these surface in the interstices of a narrative by a male writer, himself not concerned to focus on women's issues.

Note here the mention of "her hut," her separate space allocated her though within a husband's compound. Here she cooks and feeds her children and tells them stories of her choice. He tells them his stories in his. Nwoye, prefers his mother's stories to his father's—he makes his life's choices accordingly. Each of Okonkwo's wives "had her own hut" (10). Besides the shed for [his] goats, each wife built a small attachment to her hut for the hens (10). Besides stalls in the market, women work in the fields for themselves:

> His [Okonkwo's] mother and sisters worked hard enough, but they grew women's crops like coco-yams, beans and cassava (*TFA*, 3).

Their economic power invokes other public responsibilities. When a cow breaks loose into the farms, the women exact the penalty. They "checked amongst themselves to see if any women had failed to come out when the cry was raised" (*TFA*, 80).

Although women seem excluded from the gathering of the clan to discuss the question of war, the reason for the gathering is that "a daughter of Umuofia" has been killed. Moreover the final decision in war is the Oracle which is called Agbala—another name for woman; an oracle presided over by a priestess. Another all-male gathering, the Egwugwu, also makes a place for women. Their hut is decorated by 'specially chosen women', and the women's enaction of 'fear' at the appearance of the spirits is part of the ritual. The women's awareness of the spirits' true identity places them in a position of advantage, their co-operation is necessary for the ritual's success. This particular gathering reinforces the protection given a woman against an obdurate wife beater.

In fact, much more markedly than in the case of the woman in the Indian texts, the traditional Ibo woman takes her place in a range of public festivals such as the New Yam Festival and the Wrestling. For Ekwefi,

> There was no festival in the seasons of the year which gave her so much pleasure as the wrestling match. Many years ago when she was the village beauty Okonkwo had won her heart by throwing the cat . . . the greatest contest within living memory . . . (*TFA*, 28).

In other ceremonies women come into their own. There are two weddings to which considerable space is given in the text:

> Everybody had been invited but it was really a woman's ceremony and the central figures were the bride and her mother . . . (*TFA*, 77).

These, with the women, must shake hands with all the guests. When the bride appears

> All the other dancers made way for her. . . . Her brass anklets rattled as she danced and her body gleamed with cam wood (*TFA*, 82).

At the wedding in Uchendu's family, the women gather in force:

> The daughters of the family were all there . . . it was a full gathering of the Umuada in the same way as they would meet if a death occurred in the family . . . Uchendu's eldest daughter, Njidi asked the questions . . .

Not even Okonkwo at the height of his strength, exudes more sense of power and authority than does the priestess Chielo. Ordinarily a market woman sharing a stall in the market place, she acquires in her priestess role unlimited prerogatives, sovereign access to places and spaces both public and private. She strides unchallenged into Ekwefi's hut to pick up the sick child. She commandeers the village pathways forbidding others to follow. Okonkwo can only do so "at a respectful distance but even he does not dare to follow when she descends into the shrine of the great god" (*TFA*, 75).

A woman's space becomes conflated with the whole extent of her ancestral village, the place to which her body is returned for burial. His mother's kinsman Uchendu explains to Okonkwo how

> A man belongs to his fatherland when things are good and life is sweet, but when there is sorrow and bitterness, he finds refuge in his motherland. Your mother is there to protect you. She is buried there. And that is why we say that 'Mother is supreme' (*TFA*, 94).

In his exile in his mother's village Okonkwo is granted land and is enabled to rehabilitate himself till he can return home. In fact there is a deal of evidence in the traditional life as presented in these works that suggests support for the view that

> for some African women—and Igbo women are a striking example—actual or potential autonomy, economic independence

> and political power did not grow out of Western influences but existed already in traditional "tribal" life.[11]

Several critics have argued that Okonkwo's (and his society's) downfall derive from an overvaluing of male principles of ruthlessness and achievement in a traditional world that originally allowed for a harmonious balance between the male and female principle.

With works from both the Indian and African contexts the need is then to avoid premature foreclosure on the question of the disempowerment of the traditional woman who does not appear to dominate public spaces and give tangible evidence of voice and agency in shaping her world. The African woman in fact has demarcated areas of public responsibility out of the domestic sphere. The Indian woman within that enclosed space—which she can leave, when a higher duty calls—functions as a still centre around which the frenetic activity of the male figure thrashes, assisting the eventual restoration of that equilibrium and order that according to traditional Hindu belief reflects the true nature of the universe.[12]

With texts by both writers, when the traditional woman is juxtaposed beside her more modern sister 'the new woman', it is the latter who appears more nearly the victim of events and indeed of male aggression. In *A Man of the People* Edna, the educated young woman, intended as "parlour wife" to the minister appears on the same political platform but she is given no role in the proceedings, and is not even identified by name. She is attracted to young Odili, but has little choice in a struggle in which she is represented simply as a trophy in a male contest for power.

Commenting on *Anthills of the Savannah* Stratton would have it that this novel is different from Achebe's other works in that "agency is granted women." The reflexivity of this text is readily apparent, with Ikem (as surrogate Achebe) acknowledging his late recognition of women's potential. For this he thanks Beatrice. She is also supposed to have enlarged both his and her lover Chris' understanding of the operations of power. In fact the agency accorded both Beatrice and Elewa seem simply confined to the arena of sexual relationships. Elewa is first pictured at Ikem's flat being sent home in a taxi at midnight so he can get on with his work. Beatrice, a high-level Government official is never pictured at work. Her sphere of action is—like Elewa's—most often the bedroom. Not till the last scene does she assume a priestess-like role in christening Elewa's baby before a motley gathering in her flat. Contrasted with the Chielo of the traditional world, the space allocated the female has visibly shrunk—showing that the freedom that seemingly catapults the female into new spaces and roles, renders her more than ever a marginalised figure. Other young career girls are the barrister Mrs Akielo and Elsie, the University-educated nurse in *A Man of the People*. Neither is afforded more space and agency in the corridors of power, than briefly to share the Minister's bed and gratify his sexual appetite.

In the Narayan texts as well, the 'new woman' as she moves out of the traditionally hallowed domestic space is projected as a curiously disempowered figure, particularly pathetic in her homelessness. From her initial appearance in *The Dark Room* (his first work) she is destructive of the values of the traditional home. Shanta Bai—the new Insurance Agent—is given a room at the office building as an apartment. This new woman's descent into a traditional home—however fleeting—is shown to have cataclysmic effects; its traditional guardian spirit—mother, aunt or grandmother literally takes immediate flight.

While most of Narayan's works foreground male figures with women filling the traditional roles of wives and mothers in the interstices of the text, in *The Guide* and *The Painter of Signs*, this 'new woman' moves out to share part of the narrative focus. Rosie is first encountered at the railway station. Her affair with Raju is prosecuted against a backdrop of hotel rooms and guest houses. Her descent into Raju's home provokes his mother's departure abandoning her guardianship of the household shrines; his home becomes a dancer's studio. Later their lives are lived in trains and cars as Rosie steps onto the treadmill of professional success. The following exchange with Raju requires little further elaboration:

> "You are famous, you have made money, you do what you like. You wanted to dance, you have done it."
>
> "Till the thought of it makes me sick," she added, "I feel like one of these parrots in a cage taken around village fairs, or a performing monkey . . . " (*G*, 181)

Daisy, the tireless crusader for birth control is similarly a homeless, restless figure. First encountered behind a desk in her office, later, her campaigning takes her travelling in buses, trains, even bullock carts through villages, speaking in schools, homes, under trees. She is even obliged to spend one night in a tree, to escape an attempt to rape her The paradox of seeming freedom and vulnerability is well-encapsulated in that last image. Only fleetingly pictured asleep with her lover, the office is finally the appropriate setting for her decision not to marry. She gives her lover this information across her desk. The ironic humour that plays on Daisy mostly through Raman's despairingly irreverent thoughts undercuts the seriousness of Daisy's dedication. Her tremendous energy is consistently undercut by the suggestions of comic futility.

The comic irony broadens into farce in the latest Narayan representation of the 'new woman' in *The Talkative Man* (1986). The female in this novel is Commandant Sarasa, a six-foot tall army officer who has taken up residence in the station waiting-room, in pursuit of an errant husband whom she successfully recaptures. She reappears again—her husband having decamped a second time. Her explanation encapsulates the tension between domestic duty and public career:

> But alas, I could not give him enough time. I left home for the Parade Ground at six in the morning, returned home off and on, being mostly out on various official duties. (*TM*, 117)

To sum up—with both writers' works, preoccupied as they are mainly with narratives of male action, awareness of female empowerment or subjugation must be garnered mainly through resistant reading of the gaps and silences. Both project the traditionally allocated spaces as empowering.[13] In the narratives of both writers abnegation of the traditionally allocated space by the female in pursuit of public career is represented as a surrender of real power. This refraction of the traditional context as more conducive to female fulfilment could be interpreted as evidence of continuing male complicity with the patriarchy. It could also re-emphasise the need for exploring and re-discovering those elements in the native cultural tradition that have been eroded through the impact of colonialism. In any case it suggests the continuing need to attend to cultural specificities in the reading of postcolonial texts and the need for interrogating constantly any impulse towards ethnocentricism, particularly in feminist critiques of these works.[14]

NOTES

1. Works cited.

R.K. Narayan—*The Dark Room* (Bombay: Pearl Publications 1960). Abbrev. *DR*.

—*The Financial Expert* (Michigan: The Michigan State College Press, 1953). Abbrev. *FE*.

—*The Guide* (New York: Viking Press, 1958.) Abbrev. *G*.

—*The Painter of Signs* (London: Heinemann, 1976).

—*The Talkative Man* (London: Heinemann, 1986) Abbrev. *TM*.

Chinua Achebe — *Things Fall Apart* (London: Heinemann, 1958). Abbrev. *TFA*.
—*A Man of the People* (London: Heinemann, 1966).
—*Anthills of the Savannah* (London: Heinemann, 1987).

All page references are to these editions.

2. See Frantz Fanon, *The Wretched of the Earth* (London: Penguin, 1990; 1st published 1991).
3. So Helen Carr writes,

> Woman is European man's primary Other: using her as an image of the racial Other transfers the asymmetrical power relation embedded in her difference from the dominant patriarchal male. So man/woman, husband/wife, seducer/seduced, rapist/victim, can all be transferred to the European/non-European relationship, and the European right to mastery made natural.

in "Woman/Indian: 'The American' and his others" in *Europe and its Others*, Proceedings of the Essex Conference on the Sociology of Literature, July 1984, ed. F Barker et al (Colchester: University of Essex, 1985), vol. 2, pp. 46-60.

4. See Chandra Mohanty, "Under Western Eyes: Feminist Scholarship and Colonial Discourses," *Feminist Review,* 30, August 1988, pp. 61-88.
5. R.K. Narayan explored some of the ambivalences of this situation in his earliest work—*The Dark Room*—first published in 1938.
6. The terms Indian and African are used in this discussion to refer to the S. Indian and W. African (Ibo) contexts as these are refracted in selected works of R.K. Narayan and Chinua Achebe.
7. See Joanna Liddle and Rama Joshi, *Daughters of Independence: Gender, Caste and Class in India* (London: Zed, 1986).
8. This is the central thesis in Ajit Mookerjee, *Kali: The Feminine Source* (New York: Destiny Books, 1988).
9. Florence Stratton, *Contemporary African Literature and the Politics of Gender* (London: Routledge, 1994), pp. 24-25.
10. See the Appendix to my article, "Doughty Slave-Girls and Slavish Career-Girls: Representations of the West African (Ibo) Female in Selected Works of Emecheta and Achebe," *Span*, Special Issue, 36, Vol. 1, Oct. 1993, pp. 190-91. Rep. in this book, pp. 32-33.
11. Judith van Allen, '"Aba Riots" or Igbo "Women's War?" Ideology Stratification and the Invisibility of Women,' *Women in Africa—Studies in Social and Economic Change*, ed. Nancy Hafkind and Edna Bay (Stanford State University Press, 1976), p. 62.
12. For example in Narayan's novel *Waiting for the Mahatma* (1955), the heroine Bharati leads a wandering existence in the service of the Mahatma and the Indian nationalist movement against the British.
13. Abena Busia makes the interesting point that often the black African

woman's speech is signified in the text but the colonial or postcolonial critic seems unable to decipher it. See her article, "Silencing Sycorax: On African Colonial Discourse and the Unvoiced Female," *Cultural Critique,* 14 (Winter 1989-90), pp. 81-104.

14. In this connection, besides Mohanty's work cited above, see also Trinh T. Minh Ha: "Difference: A Special Third World Women Issue," in *Woman, Native, Other* (Bloomington: Indiana Univ. Press, 1989), pp. 79-116. Sara Suleri has also critiqued the practice of academic feminist writers who explore the postcolonial condition as an abstraction and enjoins awareness of the lived experience of the "woman of colour". See her article "Woman Skin Deep—Feminism and the Post-Colonial Condition", *Critical Inquiry*, 18, 4, (summer 92), pp. 757-69.

5

Second Class Citizen or Ibo Woman Warrior: Reading Buchi Emecheta's Text

The term 'Aba Riots' as against the Ibo phrase 'Ogu Umanji—the Women's War' shows how the privileging of the language of the conqueror can distort *her*story. It refers to events in the Igbo districts of Nigeria about 1929 when tens of thousands of women mustered to express their defiance of its policies to a startled British administration. The conqueror's terminology is suggestive of irrational, destructive behaviour rather than the disciplined strategy of war. Most important as Judith van Allen points out in her well-documented work, it renders women invisible.[1] British colonial investigators discovered the communication network that had been utilised but did not pursue their enquiries as to how thousands of women could engage in so impressive and concerted an action. The implications were too much for their entrenched Victorian mentality.[2]

Traditional Ibo society in fact had a 'dual sex political system' where each sex had its own autonomous sphere of authority besides an area of shared responsibilities.[3] Women settled disputes amongst women and also made decisions affecting men. They could enforce these by forms of group ostracism. To the British colonialists the Ibo system of diffused authority, shared rights and a more or less stable balance of male and female power was one they encountered nowhere else in Nigeria, not in the Emirates of the North, nor in the Yoruba kingdoms; it was wholly foreign to their own Victorian ethos.

The idea that the contact with European culture liberated African women through the introduction of Christian monogamous marriage, education, the suppression of female circumcision, is highly problematic. Rather

> to some African women and Ibo women are a striking example—actual or potential autonomy, economic independence and political power did not grow out of Western influence but existed already in traditional 'tribal' life.[4]

In Emecheta's novel *Second Class Citizen*, Adah's odyssey could be read as a re-inscription of that original attempt of Ibo woman to resist the destabilising encroachments of the colonising power into the traditional life; encroachments which had been barely contested by the Ibo male.[5]

Despite the critical commentary on the centrality of the metaphor of the slave-girl in Emecheta's work, there is simultaneously a resistant power about her female figures which, I have designated elsewhere 'the Umuisagba factor'.[6] This factor also fuels Adah's rejection of her marginalisation as doubly colonised being, simultaneously both black and female. The intersections between these two marginalities of gender and of colonised subject have been too widely explored to require comment. This Emecheta text offers a particularly instructive paradigm.

Molare Ogundipe—Leslie extends Mao Tse Tung's metaphor of Chinese woman and the four mountains on her back (where Chinese man bears three), to six mountains on the back of African woman.[7] Besides the four: foreign oppression, feudal oppression, her own backwardness and her man, the black woman bears the burden of her race and her own self-perception which is complicit with her own marginalisation. All of these motifs enter into Adah's narrative. She is born into a context in which female disempowerment appears complete. The text refracts several images of abject female subjugation, such as Adah's mother being punished by the policeman for neglecting her maternal duty. In excusing her, Pa pleads that 'women were like that. They sat in the house, ate, gossiped and slept. They would not even look after their children' (13). There is little trace left of the traditional Ibo woman with responsibilities and privileges in the political economic and social life of the community.

The signs of cultural displacement and confusion, the inevitable results of colonialism are everywhere: the U.K.-returned lawyer is greeted like a Messiah, the proprietress of the Ladilak institute is exalted because she is U.K.-trained and the Institute privileged because its pupils are not taught in Yoruba.[8] (9) The marginalisation of the female and of the indigenous culture are interrelated. Adah recognises that the female power of the older Ibo tradition has been displaced. The goddess Iboshi has been 'declared redundant' or 'she must have been in a Rip van Winkle sleep' (17). Adah's subversive attitude shows early in her lying to her mother, and taking 'secret joy' in disobeying her. It is emblematic of her revolt against this disempowered female position and prefigures her future severance from the motherland itself. Elaine Savory Fido, commenting on the works of Jean Rhys, Bessie Head and Emecheta writes:

> She [the mother] is absent, silent, yearned after and mourned. She

> is not there in physical shape, but she affects the very words we read.[9]

In a post-colonised world where the female is so marginalised, Adah is drawn to the male subject: 'when in trouble, she would look for a man, men were so solid, so safe' (6). In the binary oppositions underlying the text—male/female, father/mother, coloniser/colonised, all invoke dominant subject and a lesser other. Elleke Bochmer shows how in colonialist texts:

> dominant 'true' power—that of the coloniser—had been characterised as rational, disciplined, assertive, masculine, while inertia, weakness the disorderly was represented as feminine.[10]

Adah's first notable act of resistance is triggered by a sort of dream, "which seems to have originated from nowhere. Yet one was always aware of its existence. One could feel it . . . unconsciously at first, until it became a reality, a Presence." (7) This presence nudges her into action; it remains the central impulse behind the trajectory of Adah's progress. The first weapon to acquire in a post-colonised world is the coloniser's education. In a postcolonial world the Ibos recognised that education was "one's saviour from poverty and disease. . . . Boys were usually given preference" (9) Adah appropriates this male privilege. Her manoeuvre has all the aspects of a military exploit: her timing—'It was past midday and very hot; most people were too tired to walk the streets at this time—'; her arming of herself—since she could not march into a classroom without a slate she appropriates the piece father uses for sharpening his razor; her identifying an ally—Mr Cole; 'a huge African . . . a real black man' (11). Having arrived at the site of battle, she reconnoitres the two buildings—the Church to which she already had access and the school from which she had been excluded—then 'with her head up in determination . . . she walked down the Centre . . . looking for Mr Cole' (11). Mr Cole's alliance ensures her victory. Shortly after she decides 'she would go to the U.K. one day . . . [It was] a dream she kept to herself. It lived with her just like the presence' (15). With Pa's death, Adah's gender-based marginalisation is exacerbated. Her mother is inherited by Adah's uncle and she herself becomes a domestic slave in her Uncle's household but "Adah's dream never left her" (15).

Subsequently, each gender-based threat from the patriarchy is countered by an instinctive drawing on what appear to be culturally-conditioned strategies still surviving in the young girl's psyche. Pressured to marry because the fund for Boy's education was running low

(19) Adah resorts to a version of the traditional woman's strategy of 'sitting on a man' except what would originally have been a group show of strength is enacted alone by eleven-year-old Adah.[11] When her elderly suitors approach 'she would burst into native songs about 'bad old baldies'. If that failed to repel them she would go to the backyard and burst the bicycle tyres of the suitors.' (20) Her early mission-school conditioning cannot quell the culturally inherited 'U' factor. When at a school assembly she involuntarily acknowledges 'the Presence' and is punished for the supposed indiscipline, she sinks her teeth into the neck of the boy 'backing' her up for the headmaster's beating. From that day on no boy ever volunteered to back Adah up any more . . . (21). She earns the title "Ibo tigress." This native spirit continues strong enough to subvert the disempowering influence of Christian mission schooling. She wonders how she can secure the money for her scholarship examination:

> Didn't Jesus say that one should not steal. . . . That was the trouble with Jesus, He never answered you. . . . Then she saw the Image again. It was going to be alright. The Image was smiling, so Adah buried the money and went back home. . . (22).

Another enaction of patriarchal violence on the powerless female follows. Adah is punished by one hundred and three strokes of the cane. Yet this episode also ends with a remarkable reversal of the role of female from victim to victor. It is Cousin Vincent who is exhausted. Through the years at secondary school the Presence "existed right beside her just like a companion. It comforted her during the long school holidays when she could not go home because there was no home to go to. . ." (211).

Education gives her a degree of economic power. Obliged to marry, since a young girl in living alone in Lagos would be asking for trouble, she deliberately selects Francis whose poverty, she feels, will make him a compliant husband. Her real goal—breaching the ultimate bastion of male and colonialist privilege—getting to the United Kingdom remains ahead. Adah's earliest memories of the triumph of the U.K.-returned lawyer, and of Pa's reverence in simply sounding the name, has convinced Adah "going to the United Kingdom must surely be like paying God a visit" (8). For a while she plays the quiescent wife and mother yet in supplanting Francis as main economic provider she is already taking on the added burdens which the eroded self-image of the colonised male inflicts on the doubly colonised female. When later, total displacement—the removal from home to the colonial centre—triggers the male's experience of the extremity of his marginalisation, the consequences to the female unprotected by family and community are disastrous. In seeming to accept her father-in-law's decision that Francis goes first to the U.K. Adah recognises the complicity enforced by her mission-school education in her own subjugation:

> Those God-forsaken missionaries . . . they taught her by the bible . . . a woman was supposed to be ready to give to her man at any time . . . (30)

Yet her Ibo woman's spirit remains resilient; "All she had to do, was change the situation. . . ." The result is that where four decades before, the Ibo woman had unsuccessfully requested that all the white men go back to their own country now an Ibo woman triumphantly sets sail for the country of the coloniser[12]. She travels first-class:

> All around her were wives of diplomats and top white civil servants going home on leave. . . . It's nice to be treated like an elite, a status they were achieving . . . were not she and her children on their way to England? (37)

This valorisation of the imperial Centre is the inevitable result of the destructive impact of colonisation. In the next phase the female protagonist is obliged to work through these negative legacies—her devaluation of her own culture, her complicity in her own marginalisation. Her rejection of her illiterate fellow Nigerians comes from her colonialist educators, such "as that white lady . . . from Oxford" (43) but as Francis tells her, race is now the common denominator:

> . . . the day you land in England you are a second-class citizen. So you can't discriminate against your own people because we are all second-class (43).

Adah undergoes a process of psychic decolonisation as the Promised Land loses its promise. Her English education has alienated her from her own people and her own language: she can only respond with meaningless English songs to the pointed Nigerian songs of ridicule. She misses the support of community and family still surviving—even if only in vestigial form in the indigenous context, such as "the old woman next door who, on hearing an argument going on, would come in to slap the husband and tell him off . . ." (72) or "other mothers who would have stood solidly behind her" (72) in protecting her children.

In Francis' treatment of her she experiences the most traumatizing effects of colonial displacement. Besides the physical removal from the restraining influence of family and community, this Ibo male retains no cultural link with his past, a past in which men took part in tribal dances, age group meetings,

> . . . they would build a separate hut for a nursing wife. . . . These people could afford to build a house in which to quarrel. . . . But not in London where her Francis sat all week in the same room turning the pages of this book and that book . . . getting up only to go down to the Nobles to watch their television (171).

Albert Memmi, in his classical work on the psychological effects of colonialism shows how the colonised can turn on each other the hatred and frustration, the violence which is the backlash of colonialism. The male/female encounter as a paradigm of the coloniser/colonized is enacted in the progressive dehumanisation of both: Adah into a zombie-like passivity, while Francis is projected as increasingly bestial, even demonic.

Her awareness of "the Presence" which has fuelled her early resistance is gone;

> She started to lose faith in herself . . . she wished the Presence was still with her . . . but it seemed to have deserted her when she landed in England. Was the Presence her instinct? It had been very active in Nigeria. Was that because in Nigeria she was nearer to Mother Nature? (68)

Yet in defence of her children, her fighting spirit can still surface, as when she attacks Trudy, 'foaming at the mouth, just like the people of her tribe would have done'. (72) Both she and Francis invoke God, Christ, and the Bible to reinforce her subjugation, but when he tells her she was called 'woman' because she was made from the ribs of a man, she still has enough of her native spirit to speculate mockingly as to what Francis' interpretation of the Ibo word for woman 'opoho' would be, since it had no relation to the male 'okei'. Her experience of the conflation of the two marginalities of race and gender reaches its nadir when, her Caesarean delivery over, 'she imagines the whole ward pitying that nigger woman with no flowers, no cards. . .' (130).

Somehow her experiences in the maternity ward refuel her fighting spirit: she had "learned a new code of conduct from staying with other women . . ." (138). She experiences an awareness of female power and endurance which in the traditional Ibo context would have been readily available to the woman.[13] Christian education and city life meant estrangement from meetings of age-groups and separation from the wives of a lineage. Significantly she chooses, on leaving, to wear, her Nigerian lappa, "the one with 'Nigerian independence 1960' written on it. She was going to show people that she came from Nigeria and Nigeria was an independent republic." (136)

In the next phase—appropriately titled, 'Applying the Rules', her first move against the tyranny of Francis and the biological hazard of recurring pregnancy is her acquisition of a diaphragm. With the public humiliation and beatings that follow his discovery of her stratagem, she decides, at last, 'she could not live with such a man' (161). Like the Ibo women of 1929 who had first waited on the men to articulate the Ibo resistance to the coloniser in vain, Adah is now moved to act on her own behalf. Her next confinement is prepared for and carried through with no reference to Francis. Cards, flowers, taxi are all arranged beforehand. The female child she bears shortly after, Adah sees as beautiful and she names it 'Sunshine'. She accepts that she could not look for any support to Francis:

> She now saw this situation as a challenge . . . she had gambled with marriage and had lost. Now she was alone again. . . . She was going to survive. . . . Some day help would come (164).

Significantly the Presence resurfaces again: "the Presence that had directed her through childhood . . ." She speaks to it while stirring "peppery African soup on her cooker. . ." (164). Her passivity is over; the Ibo tigress is reawakened: 'She did not know where she got her courage from but she was beginning to fight him [Francis] back, even biting him when need be' (164). She has learnt about State Assistance from a West Indian girl who had had a baby girl by a Nigerian, but she bides her time.

Adah has consistently shown the true spirit of black feminism: 'an abnegation of male protection, a determination to be resourceful and self-reliant,' but she has yet to recognise this consciously and she is finally driven to this point.[14] The arrangement she works out with Francis none is strongly reminiscent of the balance of male/female responsibility characteristic of traditional Ibo society. Francis is compelled to work.

> She would not pay the rent because it was a man's job to do so. . . . She paid for her own food and the children's. . . . For the roof over their heads, she paid by being a wife to Francis . . . (178).

Her only debt to Francis is that he has given her children. For the African woman, motherhood is part of her female identity; though Emecheta (with other African female writers like Flora Nwapa) does not gloss over its stresses.

Her final triumph comes when she writes her book. She feels "so fulfilled . . . as if [she] had had another baby" (182). Francis' ridicule only enhances her sense of female empowerment:

> You keep forgetting that you are a woman and that you are black. The white men can hardly tolerate men to say nothing of brainless females like you. . . (184).

His destruction of her book is the final provocation for her leaving him.

Ironically, it is a white male—but a Canadian—who has assisted in Adah's decolonisation. (At the last—an Irishman kicks down the door to rescue Adah from Francis' last attack). This white male colleague confidently critiques the British system:

> He looked down on anything English. . . . He would not study for the British Library Association Exam because he did not trust the British system of education. (166)

He introduces Adah to the writings of Flora Nwapa and James Baldwin, declaring it "a shame that an intelligent black girl like her should know so little about her own black people" (166). Through these modes she learns that black is beautiful. Her colonialist-ingrained valorisation of the Centre is at last dislodged from the mind-set of this black female.

In the closing sequences, it is the resources of the modern British welfare state which appropriately provide some of the support lost to Adah, this post-colonised female displaced from the land of her birth. Leaving Francis, she is not escorted by her brother but by a British policeman.; she cannot return to the family compound but the British judge and law-court afford her security. The Ibo male sinks to his lowest depths in Francis' disowning of their children; the Ibo female remains resistant as Adah proudly affirms, "the children are mine and that is enough" (191).

Appropriately she is hailed in the closing scene by a Nigerian male voice as "Nne Nnah". Father's mother; the reincarnation of the indomitable female spirit of her people. The fact that Adah's story is also Emecheta's real-life story underlines the relationship between fact and fiction and must engender a realisation that so much of history is necessarily *her story*.

NOTES

1. See Judith van Allen, '"Aba Riots" or "Igbo Women's War", Ideology Stratification and the Invisibility of Women', in ***Women in Africa: Studies in Social and Economic Change***, ed. Nancy Hafkind and Edna Bay (Stanford: Stanford State University Press, 1976), pp. 59-85.
2. 'Not all capitalist, colonialist societies are equally sexist or racist but the Victorian society from which the conquerors of Egboland came was one in which the Ideology that a woman's place was in the home had hardened into the most rigid form it has taken in recent Western history . . .' van Allen, p. 80.
3. See Kamene Ojo, 'The Dual-Sex Political System in Operation: Igbo Women and Community Politics in Midwestern Nigeria, in Hafkind and Bay, pp. 45-58.
4. Besides Judith van Allen's well-documented article on the decline of political power among the Igbo women of S E Nigeria, see also Leith Mullings, 'Women and Economic Change in Africa' (in *Women in Africa*, pp. 239-64) for an account of the erosion of the economic status of women with the advent of colonialism.
5. All references are to *Second Class Citizen* (London: Fontana, 1990).
6. See the Appendix to my Paper, 'Doughty Slave-girls' and Slavish Career Girls: Representations of the West African (Ibo) Female in Selected Works of Emecheta and Achebe', *Span*, Issue 36, Vol 1, October 1993, p. 193. Rep. in this book, pp. 32-33. In the Prologue to her novel *The Slave Girl* (London: Allison & Busby, 1977), Umuisagba is described as a village whose women are noted for their independence of spirit, to such an extent that men are advised "to steer clear of the girls from Umuisagba."
7. Quoted in Carole Boyce-Davies Introduction—'Feminist Consciousness and African Literary Criticism', in *Ngambika—Studies of Women in African Literature*, ed. Carole Boyce-Davies and Anne Adams Graves (New Jersey: African World Press, 1986), p. 7.
8. Colonialism is not satisfied merely with holding a people in its grip and emptying the natives' brain of all form and content. By a kind of perverted logic, it turns to the past of the oppressed people and distorts, disfigures and destroys it. . . ." Frantz Fanon, *The Wretched of the Earth* (1960), pp. 170-71.
9. See Elaine Savory Fido, 'Motherlands: Self and Separation in the Work of Buchi Emecheta, Bessie Head and Jean Rhys', in *Motherlands: Black Women's Writing from Africa, the Caribbean and South Asia*, ed. Sushila Nasta (London: The Women's Press, 1991), p. 333.
10. See Elleke Boehmer, 'Stories of Women and Mothers' in *Motherlands*, ed. Nasta, p. 8.
11. For a discussion of the use of this strategy in the traditional context, see Sylvia Leith-Ross, *African Women—A Study of the Ibo of Nigeria* (London: Faber & Faber, 1939), pp. 25-26.

12. See Leith Ross' account of the Women's War in *African Women*, p. 37.
13. Leith-Ross writes of the bonding between women as follows: "more than men, they seem able to co-operate and to stand by each other . . . there seems to be something—more perhaps than merely the bond of sex which links them over a wide area so that a woman's call to women would echo beyond the boundaries of her own town . . . an intangible communion . . . so profoundly felt that the slightest stir sets the whole body trembling . . .. in *African Women*, p. 22.
14. See Filomena Steady, *The Black Woman Cross Culturally* (Cambridge, Mass: Schenkman, 1981), p. 35.

6

Resiting/Sighting Caliban's Sisters: Voice and Agency for Third-World Women[1]

Virginia Woolf's timely re-sighting of Shakespeare's sister—the female creative spirit suffocated by the patriarchal structures of a society which simultaneously enshrined the bard himself as its cultural icon—must inspire other disinterrments redolent of lost or unrecognised female potential.[2] This paper presents one such. Shakespeare's *The Tempest,* particularly after George Lamming's exploration of its significations is recognised as a paradigmatic text of colonization. It has provided a fertile source of motifs relevant to postcolonial discourse and Caliban has been accepted as the archetypal figure of the colonial artist.

> Lamming's Caliban is not just any colonial subject but specifically, the colonized writer-intellectual, the marginal person of letters.[4]

Apart from the black woman critic Abena Busia, no other discussants of the Shakespeare text have focussed on the expropriation or the shadowed destiny of the female artist doubly disadvantaged by the destructiveness of the colonial encounter.[5]

Beginning with the Shakespearean text and glancing briefly at another classic colonial text (Conrad's *Heart of Darkness*), this paper moves on to explore the possibilities of tracing the survival of the third world female (and artist) even in those contexts where her presence has been subjected to erasure, her voice apparently silenced and her power rendered non-existent.[6] In such contexts it has been argued, it was the humanitarianism of the enlightened colonizing power that liberated her. The Shakespearean text itself contradicts this. Before the arrival of Prospero (the Western colonizer) and his patriarchal reign, sovereignty belonged to the female Sycorax. Caliban repeatedly articulates his claim to the island as deriving from his relationship to his mother:

> This island's mine by Sycorax my mother which thou takst from me . . .
> Act I, Sc. 2, l. 631[7]

That Prospero's account should present Sycorax as a maleficent, even a demonic being, shows the discourse of colonialism running true to form; the colonizer-constructed Manichaen allegory that exonerates and indeed glorifies the colonial enterprise.[8] What is apparent is that before the arrival of the colonizer Prospero, an empowered female order had subsisted. This paper hopes to show that, similarly, there are traces of female empowerment in at least some of those cultures which fell victim to Western imperialism and that its erosion was one of the deleterious effects of the colonial encounter. This signification is already embedded in the Shakespearean text.

Abena Busia draws attention to the feminist implications of the silencing of Sycorax, but does not allow for the continuity of the female or of female resistance. Caliban's is the public male presence, performing the grosser physical labours that enable the colonial master to profit from his colonizing enterprise—indeed to survive in the colony—albeit with the mutterings of incipient revolt. His sisters are only to be sought in the shadows. Education, as the history of all the colonized nations show, was first made available to the males of a population, a measure whereby a pragmatic British administration aimed to fill the lower rungs of the colonial public service as well as (possibly) to create a class which would thus be culturally linked to them.

While her man sweated in the plantations of the conqueror, women continued in the main to nurture their children, indeed to ensure the physical and spiritual continuity of the race. In this text they are amongst those "strange shapes" identified as being possibly "the natives of the island." (*The Tempest,* Act III, Sc. 3) They, unlike Caliban, do not speak the language of the master; their "dumb discourse" remains unintelligible to the alien visitors. Yet the island is "full of noises," the indigene hears the noises as "sweet" sounds. Even Caliban, taught by Prospero, is now at one remove from his mother's culture—he cannot distinguish their voices, yet finds the sounds full of comfort and promise (Act III, Sc. 2, l. 130-38).

In the next colonialist text, the colonized woman is allowed to emerge from the shadows but is even more dramatically deprived of voice.[10] She speaks, but no communication is permitted her. Busia shows how this muting of the black woman's speech was achieved by Conrad through successive revisions of his text.[11] Yet several details in the Conrad text again, despite authorial controls, signify female presence and empowerment. The solitary woman appears a splendid and authoritarian figure; details of dress and gesture also operate as signifiers. Hers is the solitary gesture suggestive of defiance of the white colonizers who have reduced all of the males to death, despair or slavish indifference.

With political independence achieved in the 1940s, and the emergence even earlier of writing in English from the erstwhile colonies, Caliban may be said to have come into his own. The choice of English as a medium was problematic for some, but as some critics have pointed out, these writers' use of the language was marked by forms of 'appropriation' and 'abrogation' that stamped it as their own.[12] For Caliban's sister, historically, allowed the opportunities of English education later than her brother, this particular avenue of expression was, marginally, a later development. Yet the later emergence of the female voice in these literary forms, its apparent absence from the public domain should not be too easily interpreted as evidence of the total marginalization of the third world woman within her own society. It is only relatively recently that Western feminists have found occasion to rethink their strategies for rescuing and speaking for their oppressed third world sisters.[13]

Amongst the difficulties in assessing the degree of empowerment of the female of these regions is that Western 'markers' such as public voice and agency, economic independence seem not to have the same relevance in these cultures. Gossip, story-telling, social rituals, dress, religion, art forms, a range of practices in daily life that could be designated 'the politics of the everyday' veil other possibilities of real power. So critics like Chandra Mohanty have reminded Western feminists of this need to attend to cultural specificities in their critiques of third world texts.[14]

The Indian tradition for instance may seem particularly redolent of female oppression. The Hindu codification *The Laws of Manu,* enjoins a woman's total subjugation to father, husband and to son. Yet equally the Hindu tradition encompasses devotion to the goddess Kali; Shakti is regarded as the female manifestation of divine power. These ambivalences in the Hindu tradition need to be borne in mind if the re-siting of Caliban's sisters is to proceed as it should. It is in fact possible to discern her presence even in those male-constructed texts that historically appeared earlier on the scene.

Thus in the works of R.K. Narayan, it is the male consciousness which is foregrounded, the females remain positioned in the interstices of the narrative. The actual physical spaces allocated them are the traditional domestic spaces of the Hindu household—kitchen, shrine-room, the woman's dark room. Yet through all the novels it is they who manipulate the "politics of the everyday," remaining at the still centre of a Hindu reality while their male partners lose their way in the false allure of the world of 'Maya.' In *The Financial Expert*, Margaya's wife is positioned most consistently in her smoky kitchen, cooking for family and guests. Her tiny room—eight foot square, with no window—is dutifully handed over to her husband, first for his religious ritual, and later for his moneybags. It is from this vantage point in the home that "the mother watched the crisis developing" (*FE*, 117) the gradual estrangement of son from father. She retains voice and agency over a range of situations, from compelling her husband to conquer his petty vanity and wear the spectacles he needs to propelling him away from his business in search of his lost son. At the end, when financially ruined,

> He relaxed completely. He lay on his mat his eyes closed, his wife is in the kitchen. (*FE*, 177)

The sustaining mandalic centre has remained undisturbed; home and family with the woman "in the kitchen" remain intact. He can therefore affirm, "I am going on with it" (*FE*, 128); the source of his resilience is clear.

In *The Guide* Narayan's parable of the survival of Indian culture and religious values despite the destructive onslaughts of imperialism and modernity, the resilient, nurturant power of the traditional woman is invoked. The first overt indicator of the resuscitation of those traditional beliefs in Raju, the creature of modernity, the tourist-guide turned entrepreneur, erstwhile jailbird turned holy man, is his recall, for the edification of his followers, of passages from his mother's re-telling of the stories from Hindu tradition. In the course of drawing on that inherited store of wisdom to sustain the faith of the villagers, Raju himself is gradually reconstructed as holy man. The temple-dancer Rosie's role is no less active an agent in this process of regeneration in which the male central consciousness is represented as more acted upon, than an actor, in events.

It is the liberated Westernized woman, on the other hand, who appears curiously disempowered. Caliban's sisters must not lose touch with their island inheritance. Daisy in *The Painter of Signs*, and Rosie—despite her aspect as temple dancer—belong to this group of fevered, restless modern females who pursue the chimera of individual success and personal ambition so much the hallmark of Western culture.[16] The latest in this line, and perhaps the most extreme, is Commandant Sarasa (*The Talkative Man*), the six foot tall military commandant who bases herself at Malgudi Railway Station in her fruitless pursuit of a runaway husband. These women possess the public presence and economic independence which for Western feminists are such important markers of empowerment and yet the nature and content of that power is shown to be problematical.

These ambivalences in the Indian tradition need to be borne in mind in approaching the texts of Indian women writers. The tendency to read these too simply as protest against the marginalization and exploitation of women is to miss their more subtle ambience, to elide the essential subversiveness and resistant spirit of Caliban's sisters. Even as the practice of suttee has for long been represented, to use Spivak's words (in the Busia article cited above) as "white man saving brown woman from brown man," actually admits of radically opposed representation—no less in fact than a mode of female divinisation—these texts admit of oppositional readings.[17]

For instance in Anita Desai's work, the dilemmas of the restless, neurotic female figure are habitually discussed as representative of the victimisation and oppression perpetrated by the entrenched structures of an oppressive patriarchal system. Yet in *Voices in the City* Monisha's suicide can be inscribed as triumph rather than defeat—an affirmation of choice rather than submission. Her charred body is left as a text of victory, in the same manner as that of the young woman in Spivak's discussion who commits suicide rather than commit murder.[18]

As Harveen Mann discusses it, the novel is saturated with images of the goddess Kali and Monisha's decision is represented as a direct response to the voice of the singer, represented as a manifestation of the goddess.[19] In fact every one of the female figures shows a self-sufficiency, a resilience that none of the male figures seems capable of. These males, whether the dilettante writer Nirode, the business executive Jiban, the playboy Sunny (or his father, the solitary male from an earlier dispensation), appear rootless and ineffectual, emasculated by the corrosive experience of colonization.[20] The females of both generations are contrasted figures: the old aunt, for whom the struggle for independence still remains an inspiration; the mother, remote and self-contained in her country retreat; even the youthful Amla survives her exposure to male exploitation and betrayal through her art, her innate youthful resilience and her tie to her mother and mother's country Kalimpong—and nature.

In her other works such as *Fire on the Mountain,* the solitary self-sufficient strength of the female is again celebrated in Nanda Kaul:

> She wanted no one and nothing else. Whatever else came or happened here, would be an unwelcome intrusion and distraction (*FM*, 3).

Her little great-granddaughter is, like her, totally self-sufficient:

> Raka wanted only one thing—to be left alone. . . (*FM*, 48).

Ila Das dies by the hand of Preet Singh, but her death acquires the aura of martyrdom. She tells the grain seller, who was concerned for her safety:

> I am always alone. I am never afraid (*FM*, 139).[21]

To move to the W. African context, in the earlier written texts by African male writers, African women's roles may appear uniformly subordinated to the male. Yet even before black women writers emerged to articulate their female experience in their own works, the black woman was a discernible presence in these texts. In Chinua Achebe's classic text of the destruction of Ibo society (*Things Fall Apart*) there are inescapable suggestions of a matriarchal substructure in the Ibo lifestyle.[22] Even as the hero Okonkwo falls from his high position partly because of his suppression in himself of the softer "female" attributes of compassion and gentleness, so the destruction of the Ibo world can be traced to a gradual erosion in it of a once harmoniously adjusted balance between male and female principles which had characterised it in its pristine precolonized state. In times of misfortune a man must return to his mother's village (the place to which her body is returned for burial), as Okonkwo does, for protection and rehabilitation. As his mother's brother explains to him:

> A man belongs to his fatherland when things are good and life is sweet. But when there is sorrow and bitterness he finds refuge in his motherland . . . that is why we say mother is supreme (*TFA*, 94).

The world of women has its own autonomy, a fact that is underlined in numerous ways, such as in the wedding rituals, or the numerous other contexts suggestive of female power. There is no more impressive figure in the novel than the priestess Chielo: not even the brash Okonkwo dares to challenge her intrusion into his obi and her taking away his sick daughter at her god's behest. The final authority in all matters is the oracle, which is given the name Agbala, the same name as that for woman. The central contest between male and female powers for the allegiance of the son Nwoye is lost early in the latter's childhood when he prefers his mother's stories of birds and animals and nature to those of his father's, of conquest and heroic deeds.

As with the Narayan texts, Achebe's later works which feature the Westernized woman project her not as empowered by virtue of her English education and modern occupation but rather as much more subservient to the dominant male. She is now bereft of the traditional context that ensured her empowerment. Adrift in the modern city, she is cut off from family, age group, the community that protected her against overweening male demands. These women have lost their dignity, as wives and mothers, as also as priestesses and co-workers. They exist in these texts simply as objects of male lust. This is the fate of Edna in *No Longer at Ease* as of all of the women in *A Man of the People*. In *Anthills of the Savannah* where a deliberate attempt seems to have been made to salvage the Ibo's traditional belief in female potential, the female figures still slip into the simplistic function of sex objects, agency remains the province of the male.

Female writers of Ibo descent were, interestingly, amongst the first to emerge on the international scene.[23] Judith van Allen and others have shown how the political and economic structures put into place by the British eroded the traditional rights of Ibo women in these spheres.[24] If the modern black woman is regarded as bearing five mountains on her back—as in Molare Ogundipe Leslie's view, much of her burdens are traceable to the legacies of a colonial world that destroyed a traditional system of checks and balances on male dominance that ensured a condition of female empowerment, such as was totally unknown in the world of the Victorians.[25]

Superficially, the works of writers like Flora Nwapa and Buchi Emecheta may seem to continue the record of woman's oppression, but resistant reading of these texts reveal their oppositional character. Thus, while the slave girl motif is regarded as central in Emecheta's work, it is the resistance of the slave girl that requires to be reiterated and it is this militant spirit that characterises the foregrounded female characters in her works.[26] In her strongly autobiographical work *Second Class Citizen,* the heroine Adah, defies her post-colonized woman's destiny to acquire education, economic independence and a career as a writer despite the hostility and violence of a brutal husband and continuous childbearing. Where the male's integrity and self-respect appears totally eroded by the experience of displacement and the colonial legacies of self-distrust and self-devaluation, the female's resilience enables her to regain command of her own fate. Rather than a text of woman's subjugation, the text requires to be read as one of woman's affirmation; Adah is no 'second-class citizen' but an Ibo woman warrior.

The ironically titled *Joys of Motherhood* which could be read as a prime documentation of African woman's sacrifice on the altar of motherhood, is better read as an exemplary document of black feminism as this has been defined by Philomena Steady as "an abnegation of male protection, a determination to be resourceful and self-reliant."[27] Flora Nwapa's works similarly affirm the strength of the female in an oppressive world. In *Efuru* the woman eventually divorces two husbands, and chooses to dedicate herself finally to the service of the river goddess. It is the element of choice which confers freedom. So in *Idu* the woman chooses to follow her husband into death, deliberately rejecting the conventional choice of re-marriage.

It could be argued that in fact Caliban's sisters were never reduced to the same depths of degradation as Caliban himself. They remained out of the public eye in their homes, in their kitchens, in the temples and shrine-rooms, in domestic farms and gardens, those inner sanctum where the boot of the colonial oppressor could not leave its imprint. So they were enabled to keep the life-force of the people and the spirit of their culture alive. Where the male's experience plumbed the depths of public humiliation: ceding the public arenas of power to the colonizer, even serving in his wars, labouring in his plantations, the patterns of the colonized woman's life was less radically disturbed. Occasionally, she may have even given her body to the foreign master or cared for his children and suffered a circumscription of her own power but her spirit and soul remained resilient.

To return to *The Tempest*, as the shadow of the colonizer fades, Caliban does not—as in Lamming's reconstruction of the scenario presents it—remain 'alone.' He is joined by his sisters, the 'dumb discourse' now acquires the tones of language. The "mysterious shapes" emerge into the foreground and acquire their full aspect as the "true people of the island." Re-siting and re/sighting Caliban's sisters is an essential step in deciphering the new discourse and charting the cartography of the decolonized lands now that the clouds of the colonial era have been dispersed.

NOTES

1. Literary works from the W. African and Indian context cited in this text:
Chinua Achebe—*Things Fall Apart* (London: Heinemann, 1958). Abbrev. TFA.
—*No Longer at Ease* (London: Heinemann, 1964).
—*A Man of the People* (London: Heinemann, 1966).
—*Anthills of the Savannah* (London: Heinemann, 1987).
Flora Nwapa — *Efuru* (London: Heinemann, 1966).

—*Idu* (London: Heinemann, 1970).
R.K. Narayan — *The Financial Expert* (Michigan: The Michigan State College Press, 1953). Abbrev. FE in text.
—*The Guide* (New York: Viking Press, 1958). Abbrev. *G.*
—*The Painter of Signs* (London: Heinemann, 1976.)
—*The Talkative Man* (London: Heinemann, 1986).
Anita Desai —*Fire on the Mountain* (New Delhi: Allied, 1977). Abbrev. *FM.*
— *Voices in the City* (New Delhi: Orient, 1988).

2. Virginia Woolf, *A Room of One's Own* (London: Hogarth Press, 1931), pp. 70-76.
3. Motifs from *The Tempest* run right through George Lamming's work, *The Pleasures of Exile* (1960; Ann Arbor: Univ. of Michigan Press, 1992). The work is a kind of writer's credo. The following excerpt typifies the spirit of the references to *The Tempest* in Lamming's text:

   > Caliban had got hold of Prospero's weapons and decided that he would never again seek his master's permission. That is also my theme: a theme which embraces both literature and politics in our time. . . (63).

   In at least three chapters, the titles emphasise the dominance of this theme: 'A monster, A child, A slave,' 'Caliban Orders History' and 'Ishmael at Home.'
4. Rob Nixon, Caribbean and African Appropriations of *The Tempest, Critical Inquiry*, Vol. 13 (Spring 1987), p. 568.
5. Abena P.A. Busia, 'Silencing Sycorax: On African Colonial Discourse and the Unvoiced Female,' *Cultural Critique,* No. 14, Winter 1989-90, pp. 81-104. Busia views Sycorax as representative of the colonized female, as being representedin the person of the displaced Sycorax. Sycorax is, however, the figure of an older dispensation. Of the extensive discussions of the Caliban/Prospero relationship (mentioned in Busia's article and the Nixon article mentioned above), none explore the possibility of a sister Caliban.
6. At least two historical episodes record the appearance of indigenous women on the public stage of colonial history e.g. in Africa—the Ibo women of the Ibo Women's War of 1929 and Indian history, the Rani of Jhansi who, in 1857, led her troops into war against the British. In the Gandhian struggle against the British, Indian women were encouraged to participate in public campaigns.
7. References are to William Shakespeare *The Complete Works,* ed. Peter Alexander (London: Collin, 1978).
8. Abdul R. Jan Mohammed, "The Economy of Manichaen Allegory: The Function of Racial Difference in Colonialist Literature," in *Race, Writing and Difference,* ed. Henry Louis Gates Jr. (Chicago: Univ. of Chicago Press, 1986), pp. 78-106.
9. Alice Walker sums up the achievement of the black woman of the past as nurturer, physical as well as spiritual and cultural:

> She made all the clothes we wore . . . all the towels and sheets . . . she spent the summer canning vegetables and fruits . . . the winter evenings making quilts. . . . Her day began before sun up and did not end until late at night. . . . But when, you will ask, did my overworked mother have time to know or care about feeding the creative spirit? . . . So many of the stories that I write, that we all write, are my mother's stories . . . [but it was not the only way]. She adorned with flowers whatever shabby house we were forced to live in. . . . Because of her creativity with flowers even my memories of poverty are seen through a screen of blooms—sunflowers, petunias, roses. . . . Whatever rocky soil she landed on she turned into a garden . . .

in *In Search of Our Mother's Gardens* (New York: Harcourt Brace Jovanovich, 1983), pp. 238-41.

10. Joseph Conrad, *Heart of Darkness* (1902; New York: Bantam Classic edn., Doubleday & J.M. Dent, 1981), pp. 102-4.
11. Busia, pp. 87-88.
12. Bill Ashcroft, Gareth Griffiths, Helen Tiffin, Ch. 2 'Replacing Language: Textual Strategies in Post-Colonial Writing,' in *The Empire Writes Back* (London: Routledge, 1989), pp. 38-77.
13. See Pam Stavrapoulos, 'African Women's Fiction and a Politics of the Everyday,' *African Studies Review and Newsletter,* African Studies Assn of Australasia and the Pacific, Vol. XVI, No. 2 Dec. 1994, pp. 8-15.
14. See Chandra Mohanty, 'Under Western Eyes: Feminist Scholarship and Colonial Discourses,' *Feminist Review,* 30, August 1988, pp. 61-88.
15. In her recent publication on Hindu women, Julia Leslie shows how

> It is a small deviation from the norm which may be crucial, perhaps the way the apparently negative is transformed into something positive and powerful. Certainly the result may not seem positive to the outsider. . . . In the context of Hinduism dowry may be empowering for some women, purdah may be liberating for others. . . . It is important to realize that such choices for dowry, or purdah or sati or circumcision are being made by women who . . . see themselves not as victims . . . but as active agents in the creation of their own identity . . .

Introduction, *Roles and Rituals for Hindu Women,* ed. Julia Leslie (London: Pinter, 1991), p. 3.

16. In response to Raju's gibe that she is now famous and can dance as she had wanted, Rosie's response is "I feel like one of these parrots in a cage taken around village fairs, or a performing monkey . . ." See R.K. Narayan, *The Guide* (New York: Viking Press, 1958), p. 181.
17. For a discussion which attempts to take stock of the complexities of the

situation, see Julia Leslie 'Suttee or Sati: Victim or Victor?' in *Roles and Rituals for Hindu Women*, pp. 175-89.

18. Gayatri Spivak, 'Can the Subaltern Speak?' in *Marxism and the Interpretation of Culture,* ed. Cary Nelson and Lawrence Grossberg (Urbana: Univ. of Illinois Press, 1988), pp. 271-313.
19. Harveen Sachdeva Mann, "Going in the Opposite Direction: Feminine Recusancy in Anita Desai's *Voices in the City*," *ARIEL*, Vol. 23, 4 (Oct. 1992), pp. 75-95.
20. Colonialism is not satisfied merely with holding a people in its grip and emptying the native's brain of all form and content. By a kind of perverted logic, it turns to the past of the oppressed people and distorts, disfigures and destroys it. Frantz Fanon, *The Wretched of the Earth* (1961; London: Penguin 1990), p. 169.
21. In a comprehensively researched account of women's involvement in nationalist struggles in Eygpt, Iran, India, Sri Lanka, Indonesia, the Phillippines, China, Vietnam and Korea, Kumari Jayawardena argues that feminist ideas in these regions were not imported from the West but inscribed in their own inheritance. See Kumari Jayawardena, *Feminism and Nationalism in the Third World* (London: Zed Books, 1986).
22. See Ifi Amadiume, *Afrikan Matriarchal Foundations—The Igbo Case* (London: Karnak House, 1987) for a convincingly explored thesis that Igbo society is fundamentally matriarchal.
23. The African Studies Conference on African Women's Writing, (African Studies Assn of Australasia and the Pacific) held at La Trobe University, July 1994, paid special tribute to Flora Nwapa as a pioneer figure in the field. Invited as keynote speaker, her death unfortunately occurred a few weeks before the Conference. Ama Ata Aidoo, the Ghanian writer composed a special tribute of her sister-writer. The Conference was held in memory of Flora Nwapa.
24. Judith van Allen, '"Aba Riots" or "Igbo Women's War," Ideology Stratification and the Invisibility of Women,' in *Women in Africa: Studies in Social and Economic Change*, ed. Nancy Hafkind and Edna Bay (Stanford: Stanford Univ. Press, 1976), pp. 59-85. See also Leith Mullings, 'Women and Economic Change in Africa' (in the same publication), pp. 239-64.
25. Molare Ogundipe-Leslie extends Mao Tse Tung's metaphor of Chinese woman bearing four mountains on her back (where Chinese man bore three) to six mountains on the back of African woman. Besides the former's four (foreign oppression, feudal oppression, her own backwardness and her man) the black woman bears the burden of her race and her own self-concept which is complicit with her own marginalisation. Quoted in Introduction, *Ngambika—Studies of Women in African Literature,* ed. Carole Boyce-Davies and Anne Adams Graves (New Jersey: African World Press, 1986), p. 7.
26. A paper presented by the present writer at the African Women's Writing Conference mentioned above was entitled 'Second-Class Citizen or The Woman Warrior—Reading Buchi Emecheta's Text,' explored the militancy

inscribed in Adah's struggles for self-fulfillment from childhood through to maturity.

27. Filomena Steady, *The Black Woman Cross Culturally* (Cambridge, Mass: Schneckman, 1981), p. 35.
28. 'We can assume that they are gone. Dawn has rigged their sails; the clouds have dispersed. . . . Tonight, in his deformity and his solitude, Caliban like Ishmael is left alone.' (Lamming, p. 117)

7

The Artist and Society: Jung and Patrick White

This study falls neither into the category of literary criticism nor into the field of psychology, but into the nebulous field that appears to lie somewhere in between the two. It is proffered in the spirit in which Graham Hough contends all criticism should be advanced, that is, a kind of discourse in which "finally all conclusions are of a kind that could never finally be proved as true or false," a discourse which does not attempt to be more than "suggestive" and "persuasive, in the manner of good conversation."[1]

Some time ago *The National Times* spotlighted what is called, "The Puzzling Case of Patrick White": the peculiar mixture of fascination and respect, of hostility and dislike which his work evokes amongst his countrymen; his own peculiar love-hate relationship with his native Australia, the undoubted quality of genius in his work, and its marked religious character which appears to go so much against the grain of the contemporary outlook.[2] All this seems less puzzling, becomes in fact highly meaningful, when considered within the context of Jung's theories of the great artist and his role in society.

Artistic Inspiration

For Jung it was a deeply significant fact that about the same time that the Goddess of Reason was enthroned at Notre Dame, Anquetil de Perron brought back to the West the translation of the Upanishads, which was to be Europe's first contact with Eastern religious thought and mysticism. He felt it illustrated strikingly the rule that

> For every piece of conscious life that loses its value—so runs the law—there arises a compensation in the unconscious . . . no psychic value can disappear without being replaced by another of equal intensity.[3]

Jung felt that the contact with Eastern thought would have far-reaching effects in waking Western man to a realization of the psychic depth of his own nature. Through this he could hope to repair the damage wrought in his own spirit through the stultification of the religious and spiritual instincts which the uninhibited growth of rationalism and materialism in the West has brought about. In Jung's view, disruption in the psychic life of the community follows the same pattern as that within the individual: as soon as one of the channels of psychic energy is blocked, like a stream that is dammed, an upheaval becomes inevitable, but as long as the individual psyche functions undisturbed within a recognized system of belief, no problem is experienced. As soon as the system is found inadequate, as soon as a person outgrows it as it were, neurosis results. In the medieval world, people believed positively in a God who was their loving father, but today, modern man has lost all the metaphysical certainties of his medieval brother and set up in their place the ideals of material security, general welfare and humaneness.[4] Jung incisively analyzed what he sees as the present impasse of humanity. Apart from the rapid march of science and technology, the experience of two world wars and the threat of nuclear holocaust have radically shaken complacency. Modern man has begun to realize that every apparent advance adds to the threat of catastrophe, so that perhaps the worship of reason and materialism has reached its final stage of development. The inherent tendency towards the balancing of psychic energy results therefore in a compensating movement. Jung felt he already observed signs of a forthcoming change in the rapid growth of interest in psychology, showing that "modern man has to some extent turned his attention from material things to his own subjective processes."[5] He cites also a new interest in spiritualism, astrology, even witchcraft, and all kinds of psychic phenomena. In the context of the present study, one remark of Jung is of particular significance—"At any rate art has a way of anticipating future changes in man's fundamental outlook."[6]

Jung provides a far more meaningful interpretation of artistic inspiration and activity than does Freud. While both Jung and Freud held that the driving force behind artistic creation was rooted in the unconscious, for Freud art was no more than a substitute gratification, an expression of neurosis, while for Jung art was one of man's most important intuitive and exploratory activities.[7] This difference follows inevitably from the difference in their concepts of the Unconscious.[8] For Freud, the id represented all that was dark and diseased, all that was supressed from the conscious life of the intellect. For Jung, it was also the source of primal psychic energy, and could also therefore be the source of sustaining curative powers. As a result they also differed strongly in their attitudes to the symbol which is largely the product of unconscious processes, and also, inevitably in their approach to art and its meaning. For Freud the symbol represented a means of defence for the ego against the inadmissible contents of the unconcious. For Jung it was the natural language of the unconscious through which some complex and urgent meaning could be conveyed to consciousness. As Jung has pointed out, to reduce the work of art to something which should be analyzed in terms of the artist's repressions is to reduce it to the status of a neurotic symptom.[9] It is its quality of universality which makes art great, the personal idiosyncrasies of the artist is the least important factor. So he proceeded to his conclusion—if the work of the artist is not compensatory to the artist's conscious attitude, "the question we must answer is this: in what relation does it stand to the conscious attitude of his time?" Jung's own explanation is that

> An epoch is like an individual, when conscious life is characterized by one-sidedness and by a false attitude, a compensating movement in the unconscious activates those archetypes necessary for bringing about psychic equilibrium. This is effected by the collective unconscious in that poets, seers, or leaders allow themselves, as it were, to be guided by the unexpressed need of their time, and point the way to fulfilment through word or deed. It is thus the work of great artists comes to fulfil a definite need of the society in which they live.[10]

Erich Neumann who elaborated on this theory of Jung to provide illuminating commentary on the relation of art to its epoch, describes what this entails for the artist. It is a description which appears strikingly to fit the case of such a writer as Patrick White:

> Compensation for the cultural canon means opposition to it—that is opposition to the epoch's consciousness and sense of values. The creative artist whose mission is to compensate for consciousness and the cultural canon is usually an isolated individual who must destroy the older order to make possible the dawn of the new.[11]

The position of the great artist then presents a curious paradox. He appears to be sharply divided from the life of his contemporaries, but is in fact responding to their deepest need. As Neumann puts it,

> When the unconscious forces break through in the artist, when the

> achetype striving to be born into the light of the world takes form in him, he is as far from the men around him as he is close to their destiny. For he expresses and gives form to the future of his epoch.

What occurred in the Renaissance was the reappearance of the earth-archetype, and the dislodgment of the heaven-archetype which had in the name of religion, led to the denigration of the beauty of the natural world, and the life of the senses. Today we are again in the throes of the disintegration of the existing canon, and this is reflected in the sense of disorientation in much modern art. However, alongside the disintegration is evidence of the shaping of a new canon. As though to redress the balance of the modern tendency to over-emphasize the material and the physical, there are signs of a new movement towards re-emphasizing the spiritual and religious factors of experience. It could be held then that the emphasis on these aspects of experience in the work of such writers as Patrick White (who, as shall be seen, is no isolated figure from this point of view in the larger context of world literature) is evidence of the workings of a new zeitgeist. According to Jungian theory, it is the common openness to the promptings of the unconscious in a particular period which alone can explain the mysterious force which has been designated the "zeitgeist" of an age. It is the common force that seeks to drive all those who ever compensated for the cultural canon at a given time or shaped a new one.

Religion and the Writer

Although an article by Dorothy Green attempted to prove that Australian literature has in fact a much more religious character than is generally recognized, the work of Patrick White is generally accepted as marking a new departure in its concentration on the inner spiritual crisis and the individual religious experience.[12] It shows rather an affinity with an important trend in the larger context of writing in the West. Here, as several critics have remarked, there has been a noticeable movement towards the rediscovery of the religious and spiritual dimensions of experience, and recognition of the validity of a transcendent order in the artist's continuing attempt to impose meaning and order on his experience.[13] Often, as in the case of White himself, though these writers may not themselves subscribe specifically to orthodox Christian doctrines, their works are pervaded by Christian imagery, and explore basically Christian themes of grace and salvation. While these elements in the work of such eminent figures as Faulkner, Steinbeck and Robert Penn Warren have been frequently commented on, the trend is also apparent in the work of several other younger writers. Without wishing to imply that a new religious awareness affects all American fiction, in an interesting study of works by William Styron, John Updike, Philip Roth and J.D. Salinger, each of which has at its centre "the experience that is the apex of religious striving: the individual spiritual crisis that leads to the acceptance or rejection of God," Robert Detweiler convincingly makes his point that "a new attitude to religious in fiction . . . does in fact exist."[14] In England, writers like Graham Greene, Evelyn Waugh and Muriel Spark have all long established reputations which ensure that the label "Catholic Novelist," need not necessarily be a derogatory one. Anthony Burgess is of the opinion that "In cases where we least expect it, the elements of religion are accorded as much interest as the machinery of adultery or intrigue."[15] In the field of poetry particularly, it is a striking fact that the work of many of the great figures of the age have a markedly religious character. Apart from the giants like T.S. Eliot and Yeats, and also the later Auden and Hopkins, the stream of religious poetry continues in the work of Edwin Muir, Elizabeth Jennings, David Jones and others.

One needs, however, only to glance at the work of these poets and novelists to realize that the trend towards religion by no means represents a simple return to the doctrines of orthodoxy. Rather, what the contemporary religious artist seems most concerned to dramatize are the difficulties of a settled faith. Along with this there is a recognition of the fact that to be meaningful and relevant in the context of the contemporary world, the religious stance must necessitate an involvement with, not a withdrawal from, the realities of ordinary human existence.[16] These tendencies appear even in the work of frankly committed writers such as the French Catholic novelists Mauriac and Bernanos, or the work of Graham Greene. Although these artists formally admit their adherence to the Roman Catholic faith, in their best work the bounds of Catholic orthodoxy are often stretched to the utmost.

Patrick White then shows himself very much to be a man of his age, when, despite his explicitly avowed concern with religion and "the relationship between the blundering human being and God," he also declares, "I belong to no church but I have a religious faith."[17] His novels do not set forth any coherent set of orthodox doctrines. Rather, religion in his work must be defined broadly as a belief in the existence of a trancendental order which impinges directly on the life and destiny of the individual human being who must therefore work out a satisfactory relaionship with, and adjustment to that order. He does not set out to celebrate settled stages of untroubled belief. Rather, as he depicts it, the inevitable condition of human existence seems to be that spiritual vision and understanding is always fleeting and transient. Laura Trevelyan's difficult avowal could be placed apppropriately in the mouths of any one of White's central character's "I do believe even if it is not all the time". Moreover, White's work constantly emphasizes that the transcendental world is best approached through the objects of the actual phenomenal world. The religious spirit, as this is exemplified through the attitudes of the central characters of the novels, is shown to be intensely responsive to the phenomenal world, the natural world of bird, beast and flower as to the world of their fellow human beings. The complex webs of imagery drawn from the natural world through which White dramatizes his transcendental themes reinforce this sense of its significance to the religious spirit.

In analyzing this trend towards religion, observers usually attribute it to the artist's conscious recognition of the fact that it was impossible to draw continued inspiration from the sterile idea of a negative universe. Negative nihilistic philosophies of existence are not conducive to continued creativity. This conscious deliberate decision does not negate Jung's idea that in compensating for the onesidedness of the life of the community, the artist is essentially obeying the dictates of the unconscious. Rather, it gives added emphasis and direction to these promptings. Patrick White, for instance, has repeatedly elucidated the nature of his aims to create here in Australia, "a race possessed of understanding."[18] In an interview with Craig MacGregor, having admitted his own belief in God and concern for religion, he avers, "Now as the world grows more pagan, one has to lead people in the same direction in a different way."[19] His most unequivocal pronouncement in this regard has been perhaps his words to Clement Semmler, "What I am increasingly intent on trying to do in my books is to give professed unbelievers glimpses of their own unprofessed factor. I think that most people have a religious factor, but are afraid that by admitting it they will forfeit their right to be considered intellectuals."[20]

Yet frequently, also from White's own accounts, it appears that in the actual processes of composition, the influence of the unconscious is a factor of the first importance. In fact his first published poem was something he had dreamed of and written down on waking.[21] He has described his procedures to Craig MacGregor, "When you first write down the narrative it might be unconscious, but when you come to work it over you do it more consciously."[22] On the same occasion he stated, "I always like to write three versions of a book. The first is agony and no one would understand it. With the second you get the shape, it's more or less all right. They are largely something that arise out of my unconscious. . . . I rewrite endlessly, it's more like oxywelding than writing." It is not surprising that he should place a particular value on intuition, declaring, "Practically anything which I have done of any worth, I feel I have done through my intuition, not my mind." Questioned as to why he appeared to disparage the intellect, he says, "I don't reject reason, but I think intuition is more important creatively in the beginning . . . everything I write has to be dredged up from the unconscious which is what makes it such an exhausting and perhaps finally such a destructive process."[23] He confessed to Eiizabeth Riddell that he couldn't write a novel on some "sure fire subject I couldn't do it. I can only write the way it comes out. Or rather it half comes out. The rest is dragged out with forceps. I don't write with pleasure."[24] One recalls Jung's description of how on occasion the unconscious holds the artist almost helpless in its grip:

> Art is a kind of innate drive that seizes the human being and makes him its instrument . . . it is something necessary for him to sacrifice happiness and everything that makes life worth living for the ordinary human being.[25]

White's description of the genesis of *The Tree of Man* to Kylie Tennant could be proffered as an illustration. Having settled in Australia, he had not done any new work, till, "down by the cow-bails one evening, *The Tree of Man* began to shape and whether I liked it or not I was beginning another book."[26] When he remarks "I hate writing, I can't explain why I do write, except by saying that I seem to suffer from a kind of disease which can only be eased by writing,"[27] one recalls the artist figure he portrayed in *The Vivisector* driven to create on occasion, almost in spite of himself. Nor does it seem that over a writing career that spanned decades, that he found the processes of creation become any easier. As he told David Leitch, "Each novel is a torment that has to be gone through. . . . I work so slowly. . . . You've got to dig yourself in and get on with your work."[28]

Against the Current

Erich Neumann emphasizes that although at a superficial level he might appear to be working against the grain of the contemporary outlook, the creative man is actually deeply bound up with the life of his time, "more deeply than the common man who lives in the security of the cultural shell."[29] To the most superficial observer, it is apparent that White's education and background was such as must have brought him into contact with the liveliest intellectual and cultural crosscurrents of his time. Educated abroad, first at an English public school (an experience he heartily detested), he went on to read modern languages at Cambridge, and travelled widely in Europe and the United States. Subsequently, he led the life of a young London intellectual until his experience of the Second World War and its aftermath in England triggered his decision to return to his native Australia. Although he had throughout this youthful period remained hardheadedly independent of coteries in the intellectual and cultural environment in which he had moved, as David Leitch remarked, "White had been observing the process of decay . . . and missed nothing."[30] *The Living and the Dead* records his reaction to the sterility of English upper middle class culture, as *The Aunt's Story* glances briefly but evocatively at the chaos of Europe on the brink of war. For White, as for so many intellectuals and artists of the time, the experience of war was deeply traumatic. He told Elizabeth Riddell, "Anybody who has been in a war and who thinks, will know that it has been the most horrifying and wasteful period of their lives."[31] It seems that this experience of global cataclysm impelled a kind of spiritual stock-taking that culminated in White's return to Australia, and "the scenes of childhood, which is, after all, the purest well from which the creative artist draws."[32] Neumann emphasizes that "Only by suffering perhaps unconsciously under the power of his culture and his time can he [the artist] arrive at the freshly opening source which is destined to quench the thirst of his time."[33]

It was not that White found in his native Australia a haven from the "distressingly parasitic and pointless existence" he had observed elsewhere. In his analysis of "the Great Australian Emptiness" he mercilessly castigated aspects of Australian life which seemed to stand out particularly sharply to the eyes of the returned exile. His gibes at the "blind blue eyes" of the youths and girls, the predominance of the muscles, the addiction to cake and steak protested against a way of life that seemed to him simply physical and shallowly hedonistic.[34] The years brought no softening of attitude. He has referred to Australia as

> The country of my fate which in recent years has become increasingly abhorrent to me, which I believe it has to all men of goodwill engaged in a search for something more than a material solution.[35]

Apart from such pronouncements is the testimony of the novels, which has led several Australian critics to castigate White for what they see as his contemptuous and unfair portrayal of Australian life. Yet as Elizabeth Salter points out, White's work is "the pearl that, results from the irritation of its surroundings."[36] After the war, White's surroundings were his native Australia. Yet one has only to recollect the dreary frivolity of English middle class life in *The Living and the Dead*, or the glimpse of Europe on the eve of the war, and the American who "scrabbled on the surface of life," in *The Aunt's Story*, the restless perverted Greek Hero Pavloussiss in *The Vivisector*, or in *The Eye of the Storm* the emotionally dessicated "French" princess de Lascabanes, to realize that for White, spiritual malaise, and the need to struggle against superficiality and purely materialistic values, was far from being a purely Australian dilemma. After all, the decision to return to Australia had been taken as a result of his feeling that England had become "an intellectual and spiritual graveyard," and he has more recently reaffirmed his decision not to return because "It has been ruined." After a visit to America, he declared the people were "quite vegetable . . . one never caught sight of anyone you could imagine reading any book." New Yorkers seemed "like a herd of dark distracted animals milling through the streets."[37] The truth seems rather that White's own temperament and outlook was such as to set him strongly at odds with the currents of philistinism and materialism as he found these manifested everywhere in contemporary life. His spiritual affinity was with Blake, Yeats and Eliot, who see the malaise of the modern world as deriving from its gross materialism, its extreme rationalism and mechanization leaving no room for mystery, reverence and worship. The Australian scene provided White with a microcosm through which he dramatized a vision universal in its implications.

A Deeper Empathy

Jung's theory of the artist and his relation to society, however, also implies that despite the apparent opposition of values, there does also exist a deeper empathy. In the case of such an artist as White, how widely was his desire to find "more than a material solution" shared by his contemporaries?

A definite answer is hardly possible. I maintained at the outset that this study does not set out to be more than suggestive and persuasive. In that spirit I shall merely indicate very broadly certain contemporary developments, signs of which Jung himself felt he discerned years ago, which seem to point to considerable changes in the spiritual climate of our time.[38] Neumann, looking at modern art, observed alongside the evidence of disorientation, signs of new possibilities of harmony: "The art of our time inclines towards a radical spiritualism . . . which surges up from within and compensates for the materialism dominating the outward picture of our time."[39] The interest of the ordinary person in things psychological, mystical and spiritual has grown. Interest in psychic phenomena, in astrology, and even witchcraft are all features of the contemporary scene. Courses in transcendental meditation are advertised, and responded to by housewives, business executives and pop stars.

The Jesus movement was certainly symptomatic of a new interest in religion in some sections of the youth of the community, while the growth of hippie communes and the fascination with the religions of the East testifies at least to an attempt to seek after "more than a material solution." Interestingly, in the 1970s Australia, whose youth Patrick White had himself bluntly condemned some years earlier for their propensity to "stare at life through blind eyes" provided two striking instances of what could be interpreted as evidence of the workings of a new spirit. Drawn from the field that White referred to as the "Australian Moloch," sport, Margaret Court and Shane Gould felt moved to affirm publicly that they had both found something lacking in their lives even after they had attained the pinnacles of success, and that "only religion had filled the void."[40]

It could well be maintained today that the religious stance is no longer regarded as intellectually inadmissible as it once was, when it seemed that the march of science would reveal all truth. The writings of Popper and Bronowski have emphasized the fact that the claims of science are neither absolute nor infallible."[41] A dialogue is now recognized as possible between people of science and people of religion. The career of Teilhard de Chardin, an eminent scientist and devout Jesuit Priest, is highly instructive in this regard. The theory of evolution, once regarded as having dealt the death-blow to religion, forms the cornerstone of his thought.[42] Julian Huxley paid handsome tribute to him, for having

> Through his combination of wide scientific knowledge with deep religious feeling and a rigorous sense of value . . . forced theologians to view their ideas in the new perspective of evolution and scientists to see the spiritual implications of their knowledge.[43]

In fact a measure of the change in intellectual circles with regard to the acceptability of the religious experience is exemplified in a comparison between the attitudes of Julian Huxley with that of his equally celebrated grandfather, T.H. Huxley. Where Huxley senior could declare quite unequivocally, "I do not very much care to speak of anything (as) unknowable," and dismiss religion and the efficacy of prayer and miracles as valueless "because of the inadequacy of the evidence to prove any given case,"[44] his grandson was willing to admit, "Religious experiences are . . . ineffable, in the literal sense of the word which makes their discussion difficult. But their significance is both high and deep [as I am in all humility aware] and they certainly need re-examination and re-appraisal if their great potential value is to be recognized."[45]

All this could be regarded as the signs of the stirring of a new spirit. John Wren-Lewis remarked that despite the large number of books written to demonstrate that religious belief need not be destroyed by science, "the general public continue resolutely to believe that science has disproved religion," and so our age continues to be characterized as a secular age.[46] While the debate must remain inconclusive, I would like to conclude this section of my discussion with a quotation from Ronald Gross (Professor of Social Thought at New York University) on Humanist Manifesto II:

> There is more in heaven and earth Horatio than is dreamed of in your philosopy—Hamlet's gentle admonition to his friend is echoed, it seems to me by the widespread reaction to Humanist Manifesto II. Many intellectuals, artists and social activists . . . find this document insufficient in response to today's widespread and palpable hunger for transcendence.[47]

He cites the example of people "too important to the humanist cause because their sympathies lie with the progressive approach to world problems," and quotes one of them (Leda le Shan) on "the crippling of our psyches by our over-committment to scientific thought and the atrophy of our equally important potentialities for transcendent experience."

David Leitch's article on White was accompanied by two sketches by artist Coopes.[48] One of these especially seemed to me to convey particularly eloquently something of White's grandeur and importance in his Australian context, and even in the world at large. "It depicts tiny human figures atop a craggy peak into which the stern, accusing features of the artist are embedded. His massive strength renders the indifference of the little group insignificant yet his strength supports them, giving them indeed the vantage point from which to view their world. Whether disliked or admired the great artist cannot be really ignored because his work, in Jung's words, "comes to meet the spiritual needs of the society in which he lives."[49]

NOTES

1. Graham Hough, "The Function of Criticism," *Listener*, 25 April 1962, p. 709.
2. See *National Times*, 27 March-1 April 1978, p. 1.
3. C.G. Jung, "The Spiritual Problem of Modern Man," *Modern Man in Search of a Soul* (London: Kegan Paul Trench, Trubner, 1941), pp. 241-42.
4. *Ibid.*, p. 235.
5. *Ibid.*, p. 237.
6. *Ibid.*, p. 237
7. C.G. Jung, "Psychology and Literature," *Modern Man in Search of a Soul*, pp. 175-99. See also Jung's essays in *The Spirit on Man, Art and Literature, Collected Works,* Vol. 15, trans. R.F.C. Hull (London: Routledge and Kegan Paul, 1966).
8. For a useful discussion see Morris Phillipson, *Outline of Jungian Aesthetics* (North-Western University Press, 1963).
9. C.G. Jung, "Psychology and Literature," p. 191.
10. *Ibid.*, pp. 191-92.
11. Erich Neumann, *Art and the Creative Unconscious,* trans. Ralph Mannheim (London: Routledge and Kegan Paul), p. 94.
12. Dorothy Green, "Sheep or Goats? Some Religious Ideas in Australian Literature," *St. Mark's Review*, No. 6, June 1976, pp. 3-29.
13. Robert Detweiler writes, "the teleological dimension has returned in the form of the individual religious experience so that the critic must approach the novel embodying that dimension with a seriousness and objectivity." He also notes that a large number of inter-disciplinary studies published as evidence of "the intensity of the current dialogue between literature and religion." See his monograph, "Religion in Post-War American Fiction: Four Spiritual Crises," University of Florida Monographs in the Humanities, No.14 (Fall 1963), pp. 50-52. Ignatio Silone feels "the discovery of the Christian tradition remains the most important gain that has been made in these last years for the conscience of our generation." Quoted in Amos Wilder, *Modern Poetry and the Christian Tradition: A Study in the Relation of a Religion to Culture* (New York: Charles Scribner, 1952), p. 219.
14. Detweiler, p. 4.
15. Anthony Burgess, "The Manichaeans," *TLS,* 3 March 1966, p. 152
16. In their studies of the religious trend in contemporary literature, both Amos Wilder and Charles Glicksburgh note this fact. See Amos Wilder, *Modern Poetry and the Christian Tradition*, p. 46. Also, Charles Glicksburgh, *Literature and Religion: A Study in Conflict* (Dallas: Southern Methodist University Press, 1962), p. 54.
17. Craig MacGregor, *In the Making* (Melbourne: Nelson, 1969), p. 218.
18. Patrick White, "The Prodigal Son," *Australian Letters*, Vol. I, No. 3, April 1958, p. 40.

19. See MacGregor, p. 219.
20. Qtd. in Peter Beatson, *The Eye in the Mandala Patrick White: Vision of Man and God* (A. H. and A. W. Reed, 1977), p. 167.
21. See Barry Argyle, *Patrick White* (London: Oliver and Boyd, 1967), p. 4.
22. MacGregor, pp. 219-20.
23. G.A. Wilkes and Thelma Herring, "A Conversation with Patrick White," *Southerly*, XXXIII, 2 (June 1973), p. 139.
24. Elizabeth Riddell, "White," *The Australian*, 7, August 1970, p. 33.
25. Jung, "Psychology and Literature," p. 195.
26. Kylie Tennant, "Writer in Stained Glass," *The Sydney Morning Herald*, 22 September 1956, p. 10.
27. Pat Griffith, "Famous Author Hates Writing," *The Advertiser*, 18 November 1961, p. 17.
28. David Leitch, "Patrick White: A Revealing Profile," *The National Times*, 27 March-1 April 1978, p. 33
29. Neumann, pp. 98-99
30. Leitch, p. 34.
31. Riddell, p. 15.
32. Patrick White, "The Prodigal Son," pp. 38-39.
33. Neumann, p. 99.
34. Patrick White, "The Prodigal Son," pp. 38-39.
35. Leitch, p. 32.
36. Elizabeth Salter, "The Australianism, of Patrick White," in *The Commonwealth Writer Overseas: Themes of Exile and Expatriation*, ed. Alastair Niven (Liege: Revue des Langues Vivantes, 1976), p. 232.
37. Leitch, p. 35.
38. This "Evidence" is not cited here as necessarily implying a return to religion as such, but as broadly indicating a new value for the things of the spirit and the rejection of a purely materialistic approach to existence.
39. Neumann, p. 127.
40. "Religion Fills a Void," *The West Australian*, 7 June 1976.
41. See Karl Popper, *Conjectures and Refutations: The Growth of Science* (London: Routledge and Kegan Paul, 1965). Also, J. Bronowski, *The Commonsense of Science* (London: Heinemann, 1951).
42. Teilhard de Chardin, *The Phenomenon of Man* (2nd edn, New York: Harper and Row, 1965).
43. Julian Huxley, "Teilhard de Chardin," *Essays of a Humanist*, p. 112.
44. See *The Essence of T.H. Huxley*, ed. Cyril Bibby (New York: Macmillan, 1967), p. 114.
45. Julian Huxley, "The Humanist Frame," *Essays of a Humanist*, p. 112.
46. John Wren-Lewis, "Science and Religion," *Twentieth Century*, No. 1036, 1968, p. 54.
47. Ronald Gross, "The Hunger for the Transcendent," *Humanist*, XXXIV, 36, September 1974, p. 36.
48. Leitch, p. 39.
49. C.G. Jung, "Psychology and Literature," p. 198.

8

The Figure of the Holy Fool in the Novels of Patrick White

The death of a writer of Patrick White's stature would be followed normally, one would expect, by a spate of renewed attention to, and possible reassessment of an oeuvre which has received world-wide recognition. This has not yet happened although the present conference could be a heartening sign. One wonders whether it could be evidence of the "cult of silence" which Rene Wellek warned could descend on literary studies, as a result of the current attack on literature.[1]

Even the choice of title for paper or article (or theme for conference) can be problematic. After Barthes's 1968 proclamation of the death of the author or Jonathan Culler's dismissal of character as a 'myth,' invocation of either concept must smack of reactionary conservatism to some.[2] Raman Selden is only one of many who feel that "the terms and values that underpinned the critical writings of Leavis, T.S. Eliot, Cleanth Brooks and I.A. Richards lost their currency long ago."[3] The mood of unease with the current preoccupation with literary theory stems from two sources: the obvious divergence between theory and the actual teaching, discussion and practice of literature and on the other hand, the increasing solipsism of the theorists. Literary theory appears less and less preoccupied with literature and more and more preoccupied with itself. A spate of recent studies have attempted assessment of the present situation.[4]

Selden himself in a review of one of these works (Cain's *The Crisis in Criticism*) notes that "there are clear signs that romantic and humanistic criticism is still fighting back."[5]

The current situation however, is not simply one of a resurgence of conservatism. Despite the disquiet with the current excesses of literary theory there is a desire to recognise some of its positive contributions. Even if it seems that New Critical approaches continue to remain dominant there is an awareness of the need to explore means of offsetting its recognised limitations particularly through avoidance of a foreclosure of the many possibilities for the integration of language and literature studies.

The consensus of opinion is that in fact our discipline has not undergone radical change despite the recent avalanche of literary theory. One needs perhaps only to observe actual teaching practices in our own departments of English, discussions in periodicals, papers at conferences, seminars and particularly the practical world of authorship and publication. In a very recent discussion on the nature of the critical act, Irving Howe concludes that criticism remains essentially systematic and untheoretical.[6] Confessing himself "a little unnerved" at the frenetic activity in the field of theory he aligns himself with other critics like Meyer Abraham or Denis Donoghue who "ignore the whole thing" because "theory matters only when it determines practice" and this in their view has still not happened. David Lodge points out that despite the theorists the actual world of literary activity continues to be "obsessively author centred" as manifested in the award of literary prizes, book launchings, media interviews and the like.[7]

More important than the stubborn refusal of the writer himself to submit to being cancelled out of his creation and the continuing complicity of readers, critics and publishers in this regard is the fact that within the camp of the theorists themselves a penetrating voice has proclaimed his survival.

Mikhail Bakhtin's focus on *parole* is a radical departure from Saussurean linguistics focus on *langue,* the abstract system of rules which enables language to signify. To Saussure, the word was a two-sided sign, signifier and signified; to Bakhtin it is an act shared by addresser and addressee:

> the word in living conversation is directly, blatantly oriented towards a future answer word; it provokes an answer, anticipates it and structures itself in the answer's direction.[8]

Bakhtin's concept of language as essentially dialogue recognises, that every literary discourse

> senses its own listener, reader, critic and reflects in itself, their anticipated objections, evaluation, points of view.[9]

The novel is a particular focus of interest to Bakhtin because it involves the interweaving of various types of speech; of its very nature it is polyphonic.

Application of Bakhtinian techniques of analysis enforce a vivid realisation of the active participation of the writer in affecting the reader's response to the text and White's own considerable skills in this regard will be elucidated later on in this discussion. In the end, it is Lodge's view that "Bakhtin's greatest contribution to contemporary criticism is to have made a timely reaffirmation of the writer's creative and communicative power."[10]

In critical discussion therefore it continues to be a valid exercise to recognise the writer as a figure who, through the selection and deployment of his materials continues to affect the responses of his readers. This study will generally attempt an eclectic approach, drawing on linguistics-based approaches to literature wherever these seem helpful. As Irving Howe maintains:

> No approach rules out totally any method and no method rules out a critical practice . . . the actual moves a critic makes while engaged with a text.[11]

Reading the theorists as he suggests for "a bit of help, a lift, a clue," can be worthwhile, if it only "slows the hardening of the arteries." Compromise is constantly necessary between the abstractions of theory and the actual reading and response to literature. Culler's dismissal of character as a myth is based on the idea that it is through the writer's deployment of a limited selection of materials, descriptions of actions, and reactions, all posited of individuals, that readers conceive persons where actually nothing exists but textual devices. Yet nowhere perhaps is the essential conservatism of readers more apparent than in the continued attachment to the idea of characters as individuals. This recognition will remain implicit in this discussion of White's holy fools. In fact even the linguistic theoreticians feel obliged to recognise this process of character creation as inevitable and to concede that:

> although these constructs are by no means human beings in the literal sense of the word they are partly modelled on the reader's concept of people and in this way they are personlike.[12]

According to Fowler, both novelist and reader accumulate stocks of physical and mental attributes in the same way that police assemble an identikit picture of the different kinds of faces.[13] In fleshing out the basic data the reader brings to bear extra-textual knowledge of the world and what people are like. Some awareness of how readers respond to characters can be useful in this exploration of the recurrent figure of the holy fool and the special aura White attempts to create around it. The influence of the reader's (and the writer's) knowledge of the world and what people are like would be particularly important in connection with responses to a figure which understandably would have little credibility in our modern rationalist age.

Stan Parker is obviously invoking the ethos of an earlier age of faith that recognised the simplicity of the fool as a claim to sanctity when he reflects that "the purposes of God are made clear to some old women, nuns and idiots."[14] Stan, the central visionary figure, is at the time contemplating the spiritual affinity that subsists between him and Doll Quigley, the spinster figure in the novel. Bub Quigley, the idiot of the novel is intimately allied with her as her brother. Bub, like other figures of the simpleton in White's work is portrayed as being gifted with a special prescience, justifying the description of this figure as "holy fool."

The appellation needs to be limited to the genuinely mentally retarded person rather than applied broadly to all the innocent, guileless persons exemplifying those values of humility and simplicity that White regards as "most necessary" for the human being.[15] All the idiot figures, devoid as they are of the pride of intellect and inevitably also of social status, are humble and simple, but not all the simple humble characters are holy fools. The holy fool is a congenital idiot and must be distinguished from those regarded as simply eccentric like Mary Hare in *Riders in the Chariot*, or who become victims of neurosis like Theodora in *The Aunt's Story*. According to the knowledgeable, a low IQ by itself is not sufficiently indicative of retardation. The individual's degree of adaptive behaviour, that is, his ability to maintain himself in the community and conform to its standards is a key factor, though there is a relationship, between the two.[16] These distinctions need to be made if the subtleties as well as the developments and modulations in White's techniques are to be appreciated.

Apart from Patricia Morley's early discussion of "God's Fool," in *The Mystery of Unity* there has been hardly any discussion of this interesting recurrent motif in White's work.[17] In the sixties the general discussions of White's work by Argyle, Brissenden and Dutton hardly acknowledge the presence of this figure.[18] In the seventies, besides Morley, Bjorksten shows an awareness of this recurrent character and although he does not discuss it extensively shows an awareness of changes and modulations in White's portrayal which Morley seems to pass over.[19] Beatson's discussion of "The Tragic Clown" deals with the sense of the grotesque which surrounds all of White's protagonists even when they are at an extreme point of their suffering.[20] The divine fool does not claim special attention here, or in other general works of the seventies. The eighties have seen a plethora of general works on a variety of aspects of White's style but this particular motif has received no further substantial extension of Morley's seminal insights. Surely there is a need to take the discussion further if only because, since Morley's work, White has published at least three more major novels.

The etymology of both words, 'simple' and 'fool' reveals, as Morley rightly notes, the increasing secularism and rationalism in European culture which followed the end of the Middle Ages; "fool in particular has been given a pejorative connotation which indicates the high value which has come to be placed on the intellect."[21] White's portrayal obviously draws on the traditions of that bygone age of faith. Clearly his use of such a figure indicates his intention to denigrate the modern dependence on the rational intellect, to devalue it as a means of full understanding, to insist that in fact the intellect has failed us. Like Jung, White recognises that it is precisely the modern tendency to deify the intellectual and rational processes that lies at the heart of modern neuroses.[22] Like Yeats, White detests the 'levelling rancorous rational frame of mind' and its mechanical rejection of the experience of the numinous that is the central preoccupation of his work. With the advent of modern deterministic philosophies it requires a vision, even a courage, of a particular kind to present the fool as a vehicle of illumination.

The possible affinity between White's fools and Dostoevsky's *The Idiot* obviously requires comment. Morley notes a parallel in their uses of the figure but the point needs to be emphasised that while White's fools are definitely mentally retarded, Prince Myshkin is not intellectually deficient but is rather intended as a study of the perfect man, a Christ-like figure of charity and forgiveness. He appears retarded to a world incapable of understanding his values. As Middleton Murry notes:

> There is despair, a sardonic and awful despair in the very title. To make the conception of a perfect man tolerable to the sense of probability in the mind of the world, he must be represented as an idiot.[23]

Perhaps the cases of Theodora and Miss Hare have something in common with this figure, though White's protagonists are never projected as perfect.

Morley adheres to a much broader definition of the holy fool, averring that "the characteristics of the fool belong in some sense to all of White's characters who are presented as admirable"[24] and therefore is able to declare that "each of White's novels contains one or more simpletons."[25] This leads to some over simplification. She admits there is no obvious fool figure in *The Living and the Dead* but still attempts to fit the maid Julia Fallon into the role. In this particular novel's world of shallow socialites and intellectual dilettantes, the down-to-earth Julia seems to let in the world of ordinary human reality as she draws the curtains of the house each morning. Rather than divine fool, she is, as Walsh expresses it, "a beautiful domestic figure of the Dutch kind."[26]

Morley tends to blur other distinctions, as when she states, "White's fools may be either mentally deficient or commonly regarded as mad."[27] Mental illness is a distinctly different condition to that of mental retardation. The latter condition implies inherent limitations in the ability to perform tasks of abstraction and organisation, whereas the former arises "when an individual is in a state of dissonance or maladjustment with his life situation. As a result he may have distorted perceptions of people and the world around him."[28] In White's novels a special aura of tranquillity appears to cling about the holy fool. Untouched as he is by human responsibility, he appears also to some degree, insulated from human misery. The mad character is often overwhelmed by life's burdens. Theodora, for instance, battles with a sense of desperation and even panic towards understanding and insights to which the holy fool appears to be admitted without effort.

The earliest appearance of the holy fool is in Chuffy Chambers in White's first novel *Happy Valley*.[29] At the end only Chuffy has the key to the tragedy of the Moriarty deaths. He alone has observed Hagan's visits to the Moriarty home and could provide the missing link of motive for the murder. His testimony is not taken seriously, the jury being inclined to laugh; so the truth is never known. In this careless dismissal of the fool, White encapsulates a comment on the mental attitude that values only the rational and intellectual powers as a means to understanding.

In *The Aunt's Story*, Theodora is not mentally deficient like Chuffy. Her condition has been diagnosed as one of isolation stemming from "a peculiar honesty and intensity of vision."[30] It is Bub Quigley, in *The Tree of Man* who is the next figure allied to Chuffy. His "simple child's face" at odds with his "young man's body," immediately indicates the undeveloped intelligence. Bub, we are told, is "obviously good" and "inoffensive as well" (*The Tree of Man*, 51). It is important to note how the authorial voice is used to establish Bub's credentials to goodness and innocence. Bub alone appears untouched by the tragedy of the floods: "he alone could endure the smiles of the dead" (84). The polyphonic nature of the novel ensures that the author's ideology does not pass unchallenged. White is obliged to register the demurring voices of those who react against Bub: "many people who could crack whips and throw stones, turned away in disgust, saying it should not be allowed" (84). Despite the ironic implications that those objectors are of that shallow practical bent who would have little time for things of spiritual value, the reader would also register the limited appeal of such a figure in a modern context.

The author offers an explanation for this rejection. People turn away from Bub because of his manner of "looking into the faces of people with such candour that it became obvious he was mingling with their thoughts" (86). Later in *The Solid Mandala* it is this capacity of Arthur to penetrate into his most secret thoughts that Waldo finds so unendurable. Amy's reaction to Bub when she first meets him is one of fear and disgust. She declares to Stan, 'that Bub Quigley he makes me feel sick' (*The Tree of Man*, 53). Describing her reaction, when he showed her the cat's cradle he was making, the newly-pregnant Amy, as though she recognises some forewarning of her child's future, declares, "I began to feel myself slip, I was afraid" (50). It is only much later, when Amy herself has progressed towards some clarification of her earth-bound vision that an encounter with Bub brings her some sense of refreshment of spirit.

Bub appears the least socially adjusted of White's idiot figures. He is completely dependent on his sister Doll. In their old age, out of her love for him, Doll feels obliged to kill him, an act that leads to her own insanity. Already, in his portrayal of Chuffy, White has indicated his awareness of the almost inevitable attitude of rejection of the larger community to the holy fool. These negative attitudes are developed further in the portrayal of Bub and explored most fully in *The Solid Mandala*.

It is in *Voss* that the redemptive potential of the holy fool appears at its most striking. Voss describes Harry Robarts to Mr Bonner as "good, simple"[31] but the more conventionally-minded, like Mrs Thompson, Voss's landlady, react differently:

> Harry Robarts was always forced to wait upon the steps . . . she could not take to him poor fellow with his wide mouth and reddish cheeks . . . she could not let her health suffer by sympathising unduly with every simple boy. (37)

Harry is soon removed from the context of ordinary suburban living where he must interact with such as Mrs. Thompson. In the desert, his intuitive perceptions make him a valued member of the expedition. He alone can explain the cave paintings and is the first to become aware of the group of blacks shadowing them. His simple devotion to Voss becomes one of the factors in the latter's redemption from his hellish pride. Finally Voss admits that "he loved this boy and with him all men"

(382). He recognises how even at the height of his pride, he had always feared "the innocent eyes of good men . . . the devotion he had received from some men" (390).

Morley implies that in White's next novel, *Riders in the Chariot*, the role of holy fool is filled by Mary Hare. She notes that "Mrs Jolley condemns Miss Hare as mad . . ."[32] but also notes that "Himmelfarb is reluctant to call Miss Hare mad . . .."[33] Mrs Jolley is perhaps the most repugnant of all White's impercipient suburban matrons, while Himmelfarb belongs to his spiritual elect and is one of the four riders in the mystical chariot. Mary Hare is more akin to the recurrent nun-like figure in the novels than to the holy fool. Noticeably, she remains in the community. Despite her eccentricity, even after the decline of the family fortunes, she remains at Xanadu capable, it seems, of surviving on her own.

The idiot, "the dill," openly acknowledged as retarded by family and community, constantly requiring protective guardianship for survival in society but possessed of transcendental insights, is placed at the very centre of *The Solid Mandala*. This novel affords the most complete exploration of the full implication of this figure. Arthur is identified early in life as "One-ball Brown" and a "real dill," yet through his intuitive powers he appears to have grasped some understanding of the mysteries of being, as is shown in his fascination with the symbol of the mandala. Through his innate sensitivity and his capacity for love he develops fulfilling relationships with all those near him. Arthur's twin brother, Waldo, the rationalist intellectual, is allowed neither love nor insight. His narrowness and incapacity to love justifies Mrs Poulter's verdict on him: "he died of spite like a boil that must burst at last with pus."[34]

The complexity of the novel lies in the pervasive suggestion that part of the culpability for Waldo's fate must lie with Arthur. White's portrayal of Waldo establishes a subtle impression of sheer hatefulness and pathos. Waldo loses out constantly to Arthur in every relationship whether with family, with friends or even with dogs. Arthur's capacity for blundering into Waldo's most intimate thoughts and experiences is unendurable to the thin-skinned Waldo: "[he] had the kind of buffalo mind that could not restrain itself from lumbering into other peoples' thoughts" (*The Solid Mandala*, 191). Waldo's desperation is shown in his futile gesture of holding up a hand as he works at home as "a wall in front of what he was working at" (191) to protect himself from Arthur's intrusions. When even his workplace is invaded by Arthur, Waldo realises Arthur "was indestructible. Only other people broke" (198). Eventually the time comes when Waldo realises that "their lifetime together had exhausted him. Perhaps this was Arthur's function though:

to drive him in the direction of tears" (207).

Arthur, for his part is also led to realise his failure with the human being who is closest to him, his twin brother, and also the reason for that failure:

> 'If,' said Arthur, 'I was not so simple, I might have been able to help you, Waldo, not to be how you are.' (208)

He recognises the reason for his intellectual brother's contempt and rejection of him, his mental deficiency, and accepts a responsibility for "the hatred Waldo was directing, had always directed, at all living things" (294). He sees himself as "Arthur Brown the getter of pain" (294).

If Waldo Brown is a type of the modem rationalist, he is also a figure of the audience White addresses and whose attitude to the non-rational and intuitive areas of experience he wishes to undermine through his portrayal of the holy fool. White could hardly have remained insensitive to the implications of his own exploration, the futility of encapsulating in such a figure spiritual lessons for the intransigently rationalist secular mind. Moreover the awareness has been present from the earliest appearance of the figure, that finally for survival in the secular social world, dependence on the intuitive and non-rational powers alone is inadequate. Arthur himself recognises his need of his brother Waldo, "I don't think . . . I could live without my brother. He was more than half of me" (310). And so, after Waldo's death, Arthur is gently led away by Sergeant Foyle.

The inadequate social adaptiveness of the idiot, while integral to his innocence and purity, also militates against his value as a medium for dramatising the human relevance of the numinous experience. Through this extended exploration of the fates of Arthur and Waldo, White could well have realised the limited credibility of the holy fool as a medium of insight to the modern rationalist mind. A linguistics-based mode of analysis can afford an effective means of gaining an instantaneous apprehension of how radically divided the holy fool appears from the modern society which is his context. In semantic feature analysis of the figures in a text, a limited set of attributes which distinguish particular characters is drawn up. It results in a simple schematic picture in which resemblances and differences between characters can be instantly apprehended. In the appended chart I have juxtaposed characteristics of the holy fool in White's novels with a list of attributes mentioned by Fowler as "semes" drawn from modern realistic fiction which "reflect the cliches and stereotypes in which the society that supports that literature sees itself."[35]

The chart provides a useful shorthand for appreciating how radically divorced White's holy fools seem from the contemporary society which is their context. A kind of scale appears necessary for evaluating which of these are regarded as more or less desirable, though one's own awareness of the contemporary ethos could permit some broad conclusions. Perhaps it is those attributes which modern society would regard as least impressive such as innocence and naivety that are the common attributes of White's fools. In Arthur's case, where White completed a full exploration of this figure, there appears some ambivalence in what had first appeared its primary quality, innocence. The trait of androgyny is my incorporation and one not readily comprehensible perhaps to a modern audience. While all of the holy fools are males, White highlights with each some female aspect suggesting through this that balance of male and female attributes that in White's (and Jung's) view represents the harmonious and whole personality. Even in the figure's earliest appearance, in Chuffy Chambers, it is apparent that the young women of Happy Valley do not regard him as male. In *Voss*, the putrefying body of Harry Robarts becomes "a green woman" (388) concentrating suggestions of spiritual re-birth and fertility even in death. Arthur Brown appears as "a helpless female" to his brother, and his father is irritated by Arthur's penchant for female chores like baking bread. It is one more aspect of the holy fool that must evoke doubt and some repulsion from the more normal.

It is remarkable that after *The Solid Mandala*, the holy fool no longer appears in White's work. Morley identifies Rhoda Courtney as the divine fool of *The Vivisector* but Rhoda's acerbic intelligence, her role as sister and conscience make this seem inappropriate. Her spinsterhood places her closer to the nun-figure than the holy fool. Bjorksten suggests that Will Duffield, Hurtle's simpleton brother could be the last of these figures but admits that the suggestion is not developed:

> White only hints at it and drops it. It seems that the divinely mad as a motif in Patrick White may have died out with Will Duffield.[36]

There is no figure identifiable as the holy fool in *The Vivisector, The Eye of the Storm* or *A Fringe of Leaves*. The most convincing evidence of the disappearance of the holy fool is perhaps the appearance of the ordinary idiot, Denny Allen in *The Twyborn Affair*. Denny is simply a retarded young man. He also appears the least socially alienated of the idiot figures. It is as though proportionate to the degree of his social acceptance he becomes more contaminated by society's values. Denny is actually used (by Marcia Lushington's decree it seems) to confer respectability through his marriage with her, on Dot the rabbiter's daughter, a victim of incest. He is himself, it seems, too witless to realise the full implications of a situation the rest of the community appears to be well aware of.

He seems to represent indeed the complete reversal of the holy fool of the earlier works with his aura of being in possession of insights denied more rational beings. Far from being equipped with special sensitivity, Denny seems devoid even of a capacity to feel. For instance in the scene where Denny digs out the rabbit warren, authorial handling of detail and selection of emotionally weighted language create a particularly horrifying effect. As he digs out the terrified creature, Denny's cry "the bloody mother" simultaneously underlines his callousness and the reader's awareness of the rabbit's pitiable state, "a shovelful of bleeding fur which his matted hounds slavered and gobbled."[37] Moments earlier Denny had been speaking of his own wife, Dot, as "the mother," but there is no suggestion of the deep affinity with the world of nature, so important in the portrayal of the holy fool in this figure of the half-wit Denny. The insensitivity with which Denny shovels both mother and "kickers" "down the gullets of the ravenous dogs" could not be more highlighted:

> It's fun ain't it? You gotta admit Eddie! Fulfilled, Denny sat panting, laughing on the edge of the trench, rejoicing in his skills, waiting to return to the wife who had been made an honest woman and the child who was officially his. (*The Twyborn Affair*, 249)

White's searing irony from which the holy fool is consistently insulated in earlier works is mercilessly used here to reveal the crassness of the idiot. What the irony demonstrates is the definite withdrawal of authorial protection from this figure of the fool who degenerates thereby into simple idiot. Comparing the portrayal of Denny with that of Bub in *The Tree of Man* one notes that here it is Dot, the unsavoury daughter of the repellent rabbiter, who states 'Denny is good with the baby' adding again, "Denny is good" (*The Twyborn Affair*, 276). In the earlier novel, it was the authorial voice that affirmed Bub's goodness and innocence.

Some invocation of Bakhtinian techniques can convey an awareness of the subtleties of the White text, and how the natural polyphonic effects of the novel are carefully orchestrated in order to minimise the play of divergent ideological forces that could be antipathetic to the author's intentions. As Bakhtin indicated, the novel's polyphonic structure prevents too easy a foreclosure of meaning. An instinctive awareness of the manipulation of counterposing forces to secure the desired effect is no doubt part of the writer's skill. It is interesting to note how carefully White the author watches over his holy fools. In the case of Arthur Brown, for example, even after the worst has happened, he remains protected. For example, at the end of the novel, where Sergeant Foyle has come to take Arthur away, Mrs Poulter and Arthur are observed through the eyes of the sergeant:

> People said there had been something on at one time between Mrs Poulter and Arthur Brown. From what he saw . . . nothing of an indecent nature. There she was wiping and coaxing that nut, as a woman will cuddle her baby . . . after she has let it mess itself. (313)

Perception and speech are clearly the Sergeant's. To him, Arthur is no visionary but a 'nut,' a slightly repulsive, slobbery old man. The undermining ideology of the Sergeant is immediately counteracted by the direct speech, the passionate affirmation of Mrs Poulter.

> 'This man would be my saint,' she said, 'if we could still believe in saints. Nowadays,' she said, 'we've only men to believe in.' (314)

The sergeant is now embarrassed. Next, the author intervenes directly, significantly bolstering Mrs. Poulter's view:

> Arthur Brown got up. Filling the room, the body of this very vast old man had become the least part of him. (314)

Arthur's physical size seems to refract a sense of spiritual stature. When the focalisation moves again to the Sergeant, the psychological level of his observations has changed. Arthur has become 'his charge' and he is strangely moved as is revealed in his considerate treatment of both Arthur and Mrs Poulter:

> The sergeant turned and went out to avoid looking any longer at her mouth (315).

This segment can be regarded as a cameo performance showing White's technique in preserving that special aura that surrounds his holy fool.

The fairly regular recurrence of this figure at one stage could no doubt be related to White's conviction that intuitive and non-rational modes of perception could be most conducive to spiritual understanding. Yet from the beginning his portrayal shows an awareness of the negative possibilities inherent in such a figure for his contemporary secular-minded audience. With the detailed exploration of the figure in *The Solid Mandala* he appears to abandon this particular challenge to his audience to suspend their most deeply held assumptions of the superiority of the rational intellectual processes.

It should be remarked that after the sixties the virulence of the criticism of White for his reservation of spiritual vision for the half-witted, the rejects and the outcasts of society tends to lose its stridency. In novels like *The Vivisector, The Eye of the Storm, A Fringe of Leaves* and *The Twyborn Affair,* the upper middle-class milieu of the protagonists confers a much more worldly flavour on the novels, despite his continuing preoccupation with themes of transcendence.

In fact the later novels are generally remarked as conveying a certain sense of mellowing, a less intransigently critical White. About the late sixties White wrote to Bjorksten:

> I think I am not so conscious of Australia as Australia, in spite of all the chauvinistic rant going on at present. I don't think I have learnt to accept Australia but I endure it.[38]

Part of that endurance of and implied adjustment to Australia (and read for Australia the contemporary world), could have been his abandonment of his insistence on the redemptive possibilities of the figure of the holy fool. He indicated early his awareness of the problems of invoking a response to his particular thematic preoccupations from a modern-day audience and the need "as the world grows more pagan, to lead people in the same direction in a different way."[39]

In *The Vivisector,* the character Sid Cupples tells the story of the belled possum, its terrifying effect on the other possums who ran wildly away from it even as it ran after them. It is a figure of the ordinary or normal person's response to the congenitally retarded or the divinely mad. White was well aware that his work "sticks in the guts of the rigidly rational."[40] Perhaps his later abandonment of the figure of the holy fool could have aided, to continue White's own metaphor, the general digestibility of his later work for contemporary audiences.

NOTES

1. Rene Wellek, *The Attack on Literature and Other Essays* (North Carolina, 1982), p. 17.
2. See Roland Barthes, *Image-Music-Text*, Essays Selected and Translated by Stephen Heath (3rd Edn, London, 1982), pp.142-48. See also Jonathan Culler, *Structuralist Poetics* (London, 1975), p 230.
3. Raman Selden, *Practising Theory and Reading Literature: An Introduction* (London, 1989), p. 13.
4. See William Cain, *The Crisis in Criticism: Theory, Literature and Reform in English Studies* (Baltimore, 1984); Ralph Cohen, *The Future of Literary Theory* (New York, 1989); Thomas Kavanagh, *The Limits of Theory* (Stanford, 1989).
5. Raman Selden, "The Future of Literary Theory," *News from Nowhere, Journal of Cultural Materialism*, 8, Autumn 1990, p. 104.
6. Irving Howe, "The Conduct of Criticism: How We Do What We Do," *Salmagundi,* Nos. 85-86 (Winter-Spring 1990), p. 70.
7. David Lodge, *After Bakhtin: Essays on Fiction and Criticism* (London and New York, 1990), p. 15.
8. Mikhail Bakhtin, *The Dialogic Imagination*, ed. Michael Holquist, trans. Caryl Emerson and Michael Holquist (Texas, 1981), p. 280.
9. Mikhail Bakhtin, *Problems of Dostoevsky's Poetics*, ed. Caryl Emerson (Manchester, 1984), p. 191.
10. Lodge, *After Bakhtin*, p 77.
11. Howe, "The Conduct of Criticism," p. 68.
12. Shlomith Rimmon-Kenan, *Narrative Fiction: Contemporary Poetics* (London, 1983), p. 33.
13. Roger Fowler, *Linguistics and the Novel* (London, 1977), p. 35.
14. Patrick White, *The Tree of Man* (Penguin edn, Harmondsworth, 1961), p. 214.
15. Patrick White, "The Prodigal Son," *Australian Letters*, 1-2, April 1958, p. 40.
16. Herbert E. Grossman, ed., *Manual on Terminology and Classification in Mental Retardation*, American Association of Mental Deficiency, Special Publication Series No. 2 (New York, 1972), pp. 11-14.
17. Patricia Morley, 'God's Fool,' chapter 6 of *The Mystery of Unity: Theme and Technique in the Novels of Patrick White* (Brisbane, 1972), pp. 85-95.
18. See Barry Argyle, *Patrick White* (Edinburgh, 1967); R.F. Brissenden Patrick White, *Writers and their Work* (London, 1966); Geoffrey Dutton, *Patrick White, Australian Writers and their Work* (3rd edn, Melbourne, 1963).
19. See Ingmar Bjorksten, *Patrick White: A General Introduction*, trans. Stanley Gersshon (Victoria, 1976).
20. Peter Beatson, *The Eye in the Mandala: A Vision of Man and God* (Sydney, 1977), pp. 87-90. Other general works of the seventies: William Walsh, *Patrick White's Fiction* (Sydney, 1977); Ron Shepherd and Kirpal Singh, ed.,

Patrick White: A Critical Symposium (Adelaide, 1978); G.A. Wilkes, ed., *Ten Essays on Patrick White* (Sydney, 1970).

21. Morley, *Mystery of Unity*, p. 86.
22. C.G. Jung, "The Spiritual Problem of Modern Man" in *Modern Man in Search of a Soul* (2nd edn, London, 1968).
23. Middleton Murry, *Fyodor Dostoevsky: A Critical Study* (London, 1923), p. 134.
24. Morley, *Mystery of Unity*, p. 86.
25. *Ibid.*, p. 85.
26. Walsh, *Patrick White's Fiction*, p. 13.
27. Morley, *Mystery of Unity*, p. 88.
28. Thomas Jordan, *The Mentally Retarded* (Ohio, 1972), p. 2.
29. White never permitted the reprinting of this early work. The few copies that still survive would be highly valued as collectors' items.
30. Brissenden, *Patrick White*, p. 20.
31. White, *Voss* (Penguin edn, Harmondsworth, 1957), p. 21.
32. Morley, *Mystery of Unity*, p. 90.
33. *Ibid.*, p. 316.
34. White, *The Solid Mandala* (Penguin edn, Harmondsworth, 1969), p. 316.
35. Fowler, *Linguistics and the Novel*, p. 35.
36. Bjorksten, *Patrick White*, p. 10.
37. White, *The Twyborn Affair* (Penguin edn, Harmondsworth, 1981), p. 249.
38. Bjorksten, *Patrick White*, p. 103.
39. See Craig McGregor, *In the Making* (Melbourne, 1969), p. 218.
40. See G.W. Wilkes and Thelma Herring, "A Conversation with Patrick White," *Southerly*, Vol. 32, No. 2 (1973), p. 138.

FIGURE 1

WHITE'S FOOLS

	Chuffy *HV*	Bub *TM*	Harry *V*	Arthur *SM*
Aggression				
Materialism				
Possessiveness				
Piety				
Innocence	+	+	+	?
Naivete	+	+	+	+
Ambition				
Sensitivity	+	+	+	+
Feminity (Androgyny)	+	+	+	+
Introversion				
Elegance				
Verbal Wit				
Rationalism				
Status				
Alienation	+	+	+	+

HV = *Happy Valley* *TM* = *The Tree of Man*
V = *Voss* *SM* = *The Solid Mandala*

Adapted from
Roger Fowler, *Linguistics and the Novel* (London, 1977).

9

"Devils . . . Savages . . ." and "Nobler Forms" Patrick White's Re-invention of the Indigene in *Voss* and *A Fringe of Leaves*

Some years ago a critic described White's project as a writer as amounting to no less than an attempt on the infinite.[1] The phrase could also describe the task before any critic envisaging a commentary on even a limited aspect of his many-faceted works. Application of Greimas' actantial model of narrative analysis can provide a useful tool for exploring some of the protean possibilities of the White text.[2] Applying the model to readings of *Voss* and *A Fringe of Leaves* as re-constructions of historical events, the aboriginal figures appear as opponents.[3] They are antagonists to *Voss* the explorer's attempt to open up the hinterland, and in *A Fringe of Leaves* to the English gentlewoman's desire to return to civilization after shipwreck. [See Appendix.] As colonialist narratives of historical events texts set in the heyday of the colonial enterprise and reflective of a society built on the expropriation of the indigene the relegation of these figures to the roles of antagonist is inevitable.[4] In this context they appear as 'devils' and 'savages' (*V*, 362).

The flexibility of the Greimas model permits its adaptation to a range of ideological stances. Applied to the same narratives as post-colonial texts it highlights the centrality of the indigene to the post-colonial enterprise, seen as a yearning to belong in the colonized land, a yearning divorced from the original colonialist project (described by Conrad as "the vilest scramble for loot that ever disfigured the history of human conscience . . .") the role of the indigene changes radically.[5] Within this resistant frame of reference, the aborigines take on the aspect of "nobler forms" (*FL*, 221) as the dispossessed indigene regains something of his pre-colonial integrity. Along with an affinity to the world of the indigene the post-colonial subject becomes distanced from the original colonizing power which must now take on the role of antagonist to the indigene-elect or the new Australian.

The anti-colonialist resistance of these texts is foregrounded when compared to an imperialist narrative of encounters between opposed cultures. Conrad's *Heart of Darkness* has achieved an archetypal status as imperialist inscription especially after the African writer Chinua Achebe's rejection of the work as 'racist' and 'offensive' stemming

> from the desire—one might say the need—in Western psychology to set Africa up as a foil to Europe, a place of negations at once remote and vaguely familiar in comparison with which Europe's own state of spiritual grace will be manifest.[6]

Diana Brydon's insightful comparison of this text to White's *A Fringe of Leaves* and Atwood's *Surfacing* emphasizes their demythologizing of the powerlessness of women and awareness of the social construction of the female along with the connection between the position of the indigene and female.[7] This study will explore the mode of valorization of the indigene and other strategies which, in Goldie's phrase, work towards the 'indigenisation' of the subject.

Stephen Slemon has indicated the ambiguities inherent in the position of writers from the settler colonies—Australia, New Zealand and Canada; theirs "is the radical ambivalence of colonialism's middle ground" in that they must own to a complicity in colonialism's appropriation of the land.[8] It is a condition of their being there and "this has been their inescapable condition even at those moments when they have promulgated their most strident and most spectacular figures of post-colonial resistance." Because of this ambivalence of placement, these writings have a lot to tell to "theory" about the nature of literary resistance to colonialism. In White's work this resistance manifests itself in a reversal of the marginalization of the indigene which is the inevitable consequence of colonialism. Terry Goldie's comments on the Canadian situation are instructive:

> When the Canadian looks at the Indian, the Indian is other and alien. But the Indian is indigenous and therefore cannot be alien. So the Canadian must be alien. But how can the Canadian be alien within Canada? . . . The importance of the alien within cannot be overstated. In their need to become "native," to belong here, whites in Canada, New Zealand and Australia have adopted a process which I have termed "indigenization."[9]

Goldie sees White's work, along with Canadian writer Rudy Wiebe's, as being "arguably the most resonant literature on the indigene."[10]

White's re-construction of the colonizer as indigene-elect begins with the relationship to the land. The gaze of the colonizer on the colonized place is radically different from that of the postcolonial subject who sees the landscape of the colonized place as 'home' and not as 'foreign place'; the foreign place remains an enigma to the colonizer-exploiter who regards it with a mixture of greed and abhorrence. Observing the landscape from a distanced position on the deck of the steam boat Marlow's impressions are of a mirage, it "seemed to glisten and drip with steam," and "every day the coast looked the same as though we had not moved" (*Heart of Darkness*, 20) The alien observer cannot decipher the landscape nor decode its sounds:

> . . . every living bush of the undergrowth might have been changed into a stone. . . . Not the faintest sound of any kind could be heard. You looked on amazed and began to suspect yourself of being dead—then the night came suddenly and struck you blind as well (*Heart of Darkness*, 65).

This 'blindness' and 'deafness' establishes the alienness of the observer. Sounds, when they become audible, are 'savage discords,' 'shrieking' or 'complaining clamour,' enforcing through the unintelligibility of the savage world, its total otherness.

The postcolonial subject as distinct from the colonizer sees the colonized plan as 'home.' It is in his attitude to the land, the Australian landscape, that the slippage occurs between Voss 'the foreign bloke,' and the explorer hired as agent by Bonner and the colonial expropriators as a tool for further exploitation of the land, and *Voss* the new Australian. From his first appearance Voss reprimands the locals for their colonialist affectation and rejection of the native landscape: "A pity that you huddle . . . your landscape is of great subtlety" (*Voss*, 11). He himself has walked the four kilometres from Sydney in the heat, dismissing Laura's surprise with words that suggest the significant psychic change from foreigner to indigene has already taken place, in the conflation of the foreign place with "home": "I am at home," he said, "it is like the poor parts of Germany. Sandy. It could be Mark Brandenburg" (*V*, 11).

A polyphony of voices (Mrs. Bonner, Belle, Topp, Laura) next takes up this theme of 'the country' in the opening exchanges of the novel—the effect is of a chronic rejection.[11] Even Laura declares, "It is not my country, though I have lived in it" (*V*, 28). Voss's acceptance of the strange place as home is deliberately and formally articulated: "I will venture to call it my country, although I am a foreigner . . . and although so little of my country is known to me as yet" (*V*, 41).

Fear of the strange place—which is not home—is the characteristic response of the exile. Voss analyzes the attitude of the colonials:

> "I do meet scarcely a man here," he said, "who does not suspect he will be unmade by this country." Instead of knowing that he will make it what he wishes (*V*, 42).

In declaring the country to be Voss's by 'right of vision' (*V*, 26) Laura also acknowledges that "He is not afraid" (*V*, 28). The distinguishing element in the regard directed by the colonizer on the colonized place is a ruthless assessment of its potential for economic exploitation and profit. Marlow's disapproval of the rusting machinery, the great holes in the earth, the pointless detonations are because of the inefficiency of these particular colonial exploits and (though this is not articulated) the concomitant loss in profit. Again it is the sibylline Laura who comments on Voss's attitude: "He does not want to make a fortune out of this country like other men. He is not all money talk. . ." (*V*, 28). Mr. Bonner articulates the colonizer's ethos: "'This is the country of the future. Who will not snap at an opportunity when he sees one. And get rich,' he added with sudden brutality of the mouth" (*V*, 28). The imperial project is inseparable from conquest for profit and as Marlow acknowledges:

> the conquest of the earth which mostly means taking it away from those who are of different complexion or slightly flatter noses than ourselves, is not a pretty thing when you look at it too much (*Heart of Darkness*, 9).

The material profits of the imperial process and not its cost, particularly to the indigene, is the justification for the whole imperial project. Without these icons of Western progress the land is truly 'terra nullius,' a reading of the land that originally officially justified the historical expropriation of the indigene. The colonizer-invader reads the land differently from the indigene-elect: 'Mr. Bonner read the words but Voss saw the river. He flowed in cold glass or dried up with little yellow pot-holes, festering with green scum' (*V*, 23). Later he confronts more adherents to the colonizers' ethos in Mr. Pringle, who, supported by the young graziers "in a solid majority of tight vest cloth" (*V*, 61) assures him that "The available evidence suggests the country will prove most hostile to anything in the nature of planned development (*V*, 61). His view is that all Voss will find will be "something resembling the bottom of the sea," but for the indigene-elect in the landscape of his elective home, this becomes "a fascinating prospect." The same gap between the perception of the prosperous grazier and the visionary, the white initiate is apparent in Sanderson's explaining of the land: "The country round here is divided up for the greater part into small holdings that is to say until we reach the boundaries of Rhine Towers . . ." (*V*, 124). Voss is rather intoxicated by the sheer beauty of the landscape:

> But it was the valley itself which drew Voss. Its mineral splendours were increased in that light. As bronze retreated, views of silver loomed in the gullies, knobs of amethyst and sapphire glowed on the hills . . . "Achh!" cried Voss, upon seeing. (*V*, 128)

Even as Voss's foreignness, his German background and eccentric behaviour set him apart from the British colonial society, Ellen Roxburgh's origins as farm girl from Cornwall distances her from this same society. Miss Scrimshaw notes Cornwall is "a remote country . . . of dark people" (*FL*, 12) she adds "I cannot remember ever having been on intimate terms with any individual of Cornish blood. All my own family were fair. . ." (*FL*, 13). As British savage, Ellen is proportionately closer to the Australian indigene than to the British colonial aristocracy.

No less than the Bonners and the Pringles (in *Voss*) the Merrivales and Miss Scrimshaw acknowledge England as 'home' and are contemptuous of "present surroundings." Ellen's psychic distance from this society is repeatedly enforced in the sustained contrast between herself and her aristocratic English husband, Austin Roxburgh. She cannot pray to the Roxburgh 'Lord God of Hosts' but shares an affinity with the darker spirits of the Cornish landscape.

Almost immediately after her arrival in Hobart Town the foreign place begins to be conflated with home. She hears the sounds and experiences the smells of home:

> The scent of cows, the thudding of hooves and the plop of falling dung, filled Ellen with an immeasurable homesickness . . . she might have been driving Gluyas' cart to market (*FL*, 74).

When 'a drizzle started blowing in their faces' she declares, (while husband Austin coughs) 'I am used to it' (*FL*, 76). While Austin chooses to lose himself in the Virgilian landscape of his books Ellen frequently walks and rides into the countryside; often deliberately choosing the wilder and less frequented scene to the more orderly and settled. At Dulcet, her sensual response to her surroundings is suggestive of a sexual encounter:

> Fronds of grant ferns caressed her and she in turn caressed the brown fur which clothed their formal crooks. She was so entranced she sat down in a small clearing . . . removing the superfluous bonnet and loosening her matted hair, she felt only remotely related to Ellen Roxburgh. . . . The delicious cool, the only half-repellent smell of rotting vegetation . . . all were combining to drug her . . . (*FL*, 82)

She dreams of a sexual encounter with the Australianized brother of her English husband which is shortly after actualized. The sexual embrace as a paradigm of union with the land is an important motif in both works. White's textual strategy is quite blatant in *Voss*. In his last moments before he is finally received into the land, Voss perceives the "old man or woman" (*V*, 383), who then metamorphosizes into Laura: "Leaves were in her lips which he bit off, and from her breasts, the full silky, milky buds. . ." (*V*, 383). During her sufferings in the wilderness Ellen is materially sustained by the landscape—

> Round her the blacks were proceeding with their various duties, beneath a splendid sky, besides a lake the colour of raw cobalt shot with bronze. Despite her misery . . . Mrs. Roxburgh could not remain unmoved by the natural beauty surrounding her. Evening light coaxed nobler forms out of black bodies and introduced an element of design into what had been a dusty hugger-mugger camp (*FL*, 221).

The colonialist text inscribes the otherness of the indigene, the victim of the colonialist enterprise as a necessary mode of self exoneration. Marlow perceives the Africans whether in the varied stages of exhaustion and death or gibbering threateningly from the river bank as savage and subhuman. The recurring terms, 'savage,' 'cannibal,' 'devil,' construct the African as demonic being.[12] As the boat moves deeper and deeper into the 'heart of darkness,' Marlow glimpses 'black limbs,' 'hands clapping,' 'feet stomping' on the shore and becomes 'secretly appalled' at his total incomprehension of the beings around him. The possibility of a shared humanity with these creatures is only a cause for further revulsion.

The postcolonial text needs to re-inscribe the dignity, indeed the basic humanity of the indigene—a dignity and humanity eroded by the wounding experience of colonialism.[13] Voss's first encounter is not with faceless shadows but two individualized figures. His intuitive respect springs from his recognition of their bond with the land to which he himself is so drawn. "Their bare feet made upon the earth only a slight but very particular sound which to the German's ear at once established ownership" (*V*, 169).

White's painterly technique visually reinforces the blacks' link with the land.[14] Dugald is a thinking stick in which the ash had cooled after purification by fire so wooden was his old scarified cauterized body with its cap of grey brittle ash. Inside the eyes moved some memory of myth or smoke (*V*, 170). Jackie is 'animal life,' 'listening with his skin and quivering his reactions.' The bonding of the indigene elect with the land itself (and therefore also with the blacks) is insisted on through the visual details of the text, as in the description of Voss as he journeys through the desert:

> Blackened and yellowed by the sun he now resembled some root of dark and esoteric purpose . . . he was drawn close to the landscape. . . (*V*, 168).

In their representation as seemingly materializing out of the trunks of trees or vanishing into the earth the link between the land and the indigenous figures is consistently foregrounded.[14]

Like Voss, Ellen is made to resemble the blacks physically during the period of her sojourn with them, first in the stripping away of her western clothing, then the blackening of her skin and the chopping away of her hair: 'she had become a stubbled fright such as those around her or even worse' (*FL*, 224).

Both Voss and Ellen show an affinity with the orality which is identified as one of the distinguishing features of the culture of the indigene.[15] Voss's singing as the party passes through the forest is aligned to the singing of the aborigines on different occasions. Ellen, though unable to join in the prayerful chanting of the aborigines sings for Jack Chance as they make their way through the wilderness. In the fate of Voss's letters and Le Mesurier's poems in *Voss*, and Austin's Virgil in *A Fringe of Leaves* the European world's valorization of writing and reading is effectively subverted.

Away from the colonized world of the settlement a reversal of the hegemonic status of the white invader takes place, the integrity of the indigenous cosmos is restored however briefly. In the Conrad text the White hegemony is never subverted; even at death's door, Kurtz is able to keep the blacks under control. Originally, Voss regards the aborigines as his "subjects" though he appears to regard them with a special favour as Michael Cotter points out there is 'some imperialism' in his attitude to them. This attitude is exorcized as his relationship with them passes from partnership to dependence and thence to captivity ending with his death.[16] As the party advances into the wilderness, Voss's control is shown to be more and more illusory. Dugald's decision to return is simply announced and Voss, for the first time, realizes his own futility: "then the palms of his hands know a great helplessness" (*V*, 124). As the authority of the white man becomes increasingly attenuated, the aboriginal boy Jackie goes and comes at will. The indigenes' indifference to the urgencies of the white world is dramatized in Dugald's treatment of Voss's letters. The white man's dependence on the black to interpret the sights and sounds of the land establishes the latter's ownership. Voss's induction into the aboriginal world continues with Jackie's explanation to him of the tree platforms and the paintings of the caves. Earlier Voss is warned that goanna is food "only for blackfeller." The witchetty grub carefully placed in his mouth by the guardian elder could be regarded as the culminating point of his induction into the world of the indigene. His death at Jackie's hands is a ritual act by which Jackie finally frees himself from enforced allegiance to the white colonizer. In the moment of death White's painterly technique reinforces the suggestion of Voss's being finally received into the land: "His dreams fled into the air, his blood ran out upon the dry earth which drank it up immediately" (*V*, 394).

Judd's oracular pronouncement on Voss's end represents the final indigenisation of the white initiate: "Voss left his mark on the country. The blacks talk about him to this day . . . he is there in the country and always will be" (*V*, 443). If Voss is 'canonized', his canonization is in terms of the Aboriginal cosmogony.

If in *Voss* for a space in the text the white ruler is reduced to being Aborigines' captive, in *A Fringe of Leaves* similarly the English lady—the icon of white civilisation—becomes the slave- nurse in a black world. In the Conrad text the white woman remains pure, ethereal, apart in the safe sanctuary of Europe. In both White texts this iconic figure is displaced from her pedestal and thrown into the wilderness. Laura, through a mode of psychic participation, shares in all the privations of the desert expedition. As slave she becomes fully inducted into the Aboriginal world. Her pretences to gentility are soon forgotten as the English lady adjusts to a situation where she realizes: "The whole of life by now revolved round the search for food" (*FL*, 227). During her sojourn in the wilds she becomes even 'more dull and brutish' (*FL*, 235) than the blacks. She is pictured crawling "on all fours. . . like any sow shaking off the night and lumbering out of a fetid sty" (*FL*, 229). She is grateful for the scraps thrown to her:

> a bone to gnaw, a fragment of the beast's scorched hide to chew or suck, acts which she performed while aware of her own ugly greed and the filth which had become an accepted part of her blistered hands (*FL*, 227).

Far from being a coveted sexual object to the black men (a stereotypical assumption of colonialist inscribed texts), they "paid little attention to a woman of unprepossessing colour" (*FL*, 238). Her induction into the indigenous world progresses as she becomes a contributor to the foodstore of the tribe:

> As she developed an aptitude for climbing trees she was sent in search of birds' nests in addition to opossum. . . . Sometimes she found honeycombs (*FL*, 238).

As with Voss, a ritualized act of communion marks the climax of her initiation into the innermost mysteries of the aboriginal world. The sacramental significance of Ellen's participation in the rites of cannibalism have been discussed by several critics.[17]

Where the Conradian narrative never permits human interaction between colonizer master and colonized subject, Ellen, even while confined to slave status, is permitted to share the tribes' human tragedies. At the death of the child her unwelcome charge, "for the first time since the meeting on the beach, the captive and her masters, especially the women were united in a common humanity'" (*FL*, 234). Voss, from their first meeting, clings to the idea of a special bond between himself and the blacks. In this text's reversal of black/white power relations of colonized society perhaps the most remarkable feature is the social mobility allowed the white initiate who moves from captive slave to nurse and formally-acquired wife to Turrwan medicine-man to the clan. The so-called primitive indigenes' capacity to hold the slave and goddess-figure in the same gaze (Voss too though captive remains aligned with divinity) shows an avoidance of simpler binary oppositions so characteristic of the colonized culture. Difference in the indigenous world it would appear is an impulse to awe; in the white culture it is denigrated as characteristic of the conquered and humiliated 'other.'

Finally for the subject figures of these postcolonial narratives, Voss and Ellen, the contact with the indigene becomes a mode of psychic growth, a progression towards an expanded vision. For both it promises spiritual and physical survival. The fact of physical death is shown to be immaterial to Voss, whose legend continues to be told, "he is there in the country" (*V*, 443). Terry Goldie, comparing White and the Canadian writer Rudy Wiebe finds that both writers are concerned, along with "a search for individuation usually traced along mystical patterns" with "a search for country." He concludes therefore, "It should not be surprising then that Wiebe and White have often turned to the semiotic field of the indigene with its long established signifiers for the spiritual and the national."[18] For Kurtz as for Marlow the contact with the 'other' can only be summed up in Kurtz's last words "The horror. The horror."

White's texts read as postcolonial narratives could be held to refract the growth of consciousness where the psyche of the settler/invader expands into the awareness of the settler/indigene. The latter term unties the crippling and reductive binary oppositions of the relation between colonizer and colonized; it invokes their connecting bond the land on which the continued survival of both depend. In the post-colonial texts the colonized landscape becomes not 'there' but 'here,' the 'foreign place' has become 'home.' The gaze that regards the indigene initially as 'devil' or 'savage' must also discern the 'nobler form' if only because of his first ownership of the land and indeed, in terms of the Aboriginal cosmogony his being the land itself. The later—or incipient-indigenization of the settler-invader is perhaps better inscribed in the descriptor settler-indigene. This latter description excises the implication of continued complicity with the colonial power and emphasizes rather a bonding to the land and through it to its indigenous people.

NOTES

1. "Attempting the Infinite," *The Times Literary Supplement,* 15 December 1961, pp. 889-91.
2. See Ch. X—Reflections on Actantial Models, particularly pp. 207-9. A.J. Greimas, *Structural Semantics. An Attempt at a Method*, trans. Daniele McDowell, Ronald Schliefer and Alan Velie (London: Univ. Of Nebraska Press, 1983). In constructing a narrative grammar, Greimas subordinates characters by calling them actants. He distinguishes 'between acteurs and actants.' The former can have specific qualities varying in different narratives, the latter are general categories underlying all narratives. Both can include not only human beings but while acteurs are numerous, Greimas' model has six actants only: sender—object—receiver—helper—subject—opponent.
3. *Riders in the Chariot*, White's third novel in which an Aboriginal character is one of the four central figures will not be considered in this study. Alf

Dubbo is part-Aboriginal, and a contemporary figure. His inclusion would have necessarily involved a number of additional variables which could not be adequately dealt within the confines of this paper. J.J.Healy sees this novel as marking "the highest point in the European consciousness of the Aborigine in Australian literature." See his *Literature and the Aborigine in Australia* (University of Queensland Press, 1989), p. 205.

4. Both novels draw on a range of historical materials. See Jill Ward, 'Patrick White's *A Fringe of Leaves*: History and Fiction,' ALS, VIII, 1978, pp. 402-18; Marcel Aurousseau, 'The Identity of Voss,' *Meanjin*, XVIII, April 1958, pp. 85-87. [All page refs. are to the Penguin editions of these works which will be abbreviated in this text as *FL* and *V*].
5. From his essay on 'Geography and some explorers' (1924). Quoted in Ian Watt, *Conrad in the Nineteenth Century* (Chatto and Windus, London, 1980), p.140.
6. Chinua Achebe, 'An Image of Africa,' *The Massachusetts Review*, 18, No. 4 (1977), p. 783. The edition of Conrad's novel referred to in this study is *Heart of Darkness and The Secret Sharer* (Bantam Classic edition, New York, 1981).
7. Diana Brydon, "'The Thematic Ancestor,' Joseph Conrad, Patrick White and Margaret Atwood," *WLWE*, XXIV, No. 2 (1984), pp. 386-97.
8. Stephen Slemon, 'Unsettling the Empire: Resistance Theory for the Second World,' *WLWE*, Vol. 30, No. 2 (1990), pp. 30-41.
9. Terry Goldie, *Fear and Temptation, The Image of the Indigene in Canadian, Australian and New Zealand Literatures* (London: McGill-Queen's University Press, 1989), pp. 12-13.
10. Goldie, p. 192.
11. Attitudes to the country: "'Ah! This country" sighed his wife, who remembered others and feared for her complexion' (*Voss*, p. 28);
    Belle: "I would not like to ride very far into it . . . and meet a lot of blacks and deserts and rocks and skeletons . . ." (*Voss*, p. 28);
    Topp: "It is no country of mine . . . except by the unfortunate accident of my being here" (*Voss*, p. 40).
12. Flemming Brahms, "Entering Our Own Ignorance: Subject-Object Relations in Commonwealth Literature," *WLWE*, 21.2 (Summer, 1982), pp. 233-34.
13. Frantz Fanon has written of the extreme destructiveness of the experience of colonialism: "Colonialism is not satisfied merely with holding a people in its grip and emptying the native's brain of all form and content. By a kind of perverted logic, it turns to the past of the oppressed people and distorts, disfigures and destroys it. . . ." *The Wretched of the Earth* (1965), p.170.
14. Note the description of the first appearance of the Aborigines in the desert: "Other figures were beginning to appear, their shadows first, followed by a suggestion of skin wedded to the trunk of a tree" (*Voss*, p. 191).

    Again later: ". . . a party of blacks appeared first as sheets of shy bark glimpsed between the trunks of trees, but always drifting, until finally they halted in human form upon the outskirts of the camp." (*Voss*, p. 204)

The equation of man-plant-animal-place should not be regarded as derogatory of the status of Aboriginal man. All of these are also finally interchangeable with the ancestral beings who are believed to have brought the land itself and its features into existence as they wandered through it in the Dreamtime. Most anthropological investigations, while allowing for the great variety that subsists among the different moieties concur that generally for Aborigines:

> The human, plant, animal and spiritual inhabitants of their cosmos are perceived as co-existing as one, within the all-embracing canopy provided by the founding of the Dreamtime.

R. Tonkinson, *The Mardujara Aborigines: Living the Dream in Australia's Desert* (New York: Holt, Rinehart and Winston, 1978), p. 115. See also, Berndt, Ronald M. and Catherine H. Ch VII, 'Religious Mythology' in *The World of the First Australians*; (Sydney; Ure Smith, 1964), pp. 185-216. The chapter includes a recounting of several myths to illustrate such ideas as the following:

> In the Western Desert, people say there are still wandering 'djugurba' beings like those among the Dieri, partly human, partly animal, reptile, bird and so on, but in the myths they are thought of as mainly human. (Berndt, p. 205)

15. Goldie, pp. 107-26.
16. See Michael Cotter on the 'imperialism' of Voss's attitude in 'Fragmentation, Reconstitution and the Colonial Experience: The Aborigine in Patrick White's Fiction,' in *South Pacific Images*, ed. Chris Tiffin (St. Lucia; South Pacific Association for Commonwealth Literature on Language Studies, 1978), p. 178. Cotter's early study sensitively explores the coming together in White's work of the two cultures—white and aboriginal.
17. See Patricia Morley, 'Patrick White's *A Fringe of Leaves*: Journey to Tintagel,' *WLWE*, XXI, 1982, pp. 303-15, or Goldie, pp. 202-3.
18. Goldie, p. 192.

Appendix

Fig.1A Voss—Post Colonial Narrative

Sender	*Subject*	*Helper*
Colonized Land	Voss	Indigene
Receiver	*Object*	*Opponent*
Voss—New Australian	Indigenization	Colonialism

Fig. 1B ***A Fringe of Leaves*—Post Colonial Narrative**

Sender	*Subject*	*Helper*
Colonized Land	Ellen	Indigene
Receiver	*Object*	*Opponent*
Ellen—New Australia	Indigenization	Colonialism

Fig. 2A ***Voss*— 'Historical' Narrative**

Sender	*Subject*	*Helper*
Colonizing Power	Voss	Colonialism
Receiver	*Object*	*Opponent*
Voss—German explorer	Hegemony of Colonizing Power	Indigene

Fig. 2B ***A Fringe of Leaves*—'Historical' Narrative**

Sender	*Subject*	*Helper*
Colonizing Power	Ellen	Colonialism
Receiver	*Object*	*Opponent*
Ellen—English lady	Hegemony of Colonizing Power	Indigene

10

Asian Writing in Australia

Exploring the discourse of Orientalism, Edward Said mentions a range of strategies which have operated in literary texts to construct the Orient as Europe's 'Other.' Amongst these are 'strategic location'—authorial position with regard to the material written about; the 'narrative voice' adopted; the 'kinds of images, themes, motifs that circulate in the text.'[1] These strategies have delivered 'representations of the Orient,' the end result of which has been a discourse in which the Orient is established as 'lamentably alien.'

Conrad's *Heart of Darkness* is evidence of how such devices work towards dehumanising, indeed towards demonising the African.[2] I hope to show in this Paper, how these devices can also work towards exorcising alterity and re-aligning this discourse of 'otherness.' In Conrad's text, the narrator, Marlow, views the African landscape and the African from a distanced position on the steamboat. The Africans are glimpsed as a medley of disembodied limbs, shadowy, barely human. Those working on the boat make no compensatory gain in humanity. These subsist on rotting hippo flesh, their cannibal instincts suppressed by grace of the white presence. The motif of food is important and will be referred to again. Note how often terms of racial abuse refer to the eating of taboo food by those of a different culture. Epithets such as 'savage' and 'cannibal' reinforce the impression of beings totally alien to the civilised European gaze.[3] Add to these details, the total absence of a shared language and the strangeness of the environing landscape and the Conrad text provides a paradigm for the construction of racial otherness in narrative. It shows how the 'real' Orient is excluded in Orientalist narrative:

> Orientals were rarely seen or looked at: they were seen through, analysed not as citizens or alien people but as problems to be solved or confined or (as the colonial powers openly coveted their territory) taken over.[4]

Australian writers of the past have resorted to Orientalist strategies in construction of the Asian, particularly the Chinese. The burgeoning sense of national identity of the 1890s was tied to ideas of racial homogeneity though women and convicts were also excluded:

> All white men who come to these shores with a clean record. . . . No nigger, no Chinaman, no lascar, no kanaka, no purveyor of cheap coloured labour is an Australian. . .

So runs a pronouncement from *The Bulletin* of the period.[5]

Alison Broinowski has commented incisively on Australian constructions of the Asian: Besides literature and film, cartoonists produced 'images of Asians as a pestiferous insect plague, an Oriental dragon, or a Mongolian octopus, whose talents wormed into every hallowed Australian institution.'[6] Fanon, Memmi and latter-day critics like Jan-Mohammed have shown how the deliberate denigration of the dignity and humanity of the non-European 'Other' was the necessary precondition for the self-exoneration of the imperialist West.[7] The gulf of racial and cultural difference that yawns between Asian and European as the discourse of Orientalism constructs it, is of mythic proportions. For the writer from an Asian background the experience of exile and alienation would be articulated, one would expect, in more traumatic terms, than in the work of writers from Greek, Italian and other European origins. These latter share with Anglo-Celtic Australians a complicity with the Imperialist project that marks all white residents in settler cultures.[8] They too, therefore must share in the dehumanising gaze that Europe turns on its Other—the Orient.

For Asians (as for Australians) Australia is an European outpost in Asia. For the White Australian the image of racial otherness inheres in the Asian, the Oriental. The Asian's aspect as Other is underlined by the obvious physical difference so strikingly apparent in the sketch of an 1890s scene of the Circular Quay in Sydney by Norman Lindsay.[9] More recent Australian writing, such as the novels by Drewe, D'Alpuget and Koch—despite the titles of novels which seem to invoke deliberately the stereotypes of Asian menace and mystery have shown a tendency to interrogate the patterns of Orientalist-devised binary oppositions—oppressed/free, civilised/savage.[10] In the Drewe work, for example, Cullen is acutely aware of how he must appear to the locals—his great bulk, his physical clumsiness. The D'Alpuget heroine is able to view Minou's suicide as possibly a redemptive act, through the eyes of her Indian lover, Kannan. Billy Kwan—in Koch's work, is a living metaphor of the hybridised consciousness. The encounter with Billy forces Hamilton out of his stereotypical Western attitude to the Orient as simply a site for individual self-aggrandisement. What these works evidence is the development of a new hybridity in the Australian consciousness.

It is perhaps most markedly evident in the newly-emergent writing of writers of Asian extraction in Australia. The 'newness' of this phenomenon of Asian writing in Australia hardly requires explanation for anyone acquainted with the politics of the White Australia policy. In fact even the latest collection of critical pronouncements on multi-cultural writing, elicits barely a nod of acknowledgment in the direction of these writers.[11] As a critic, perhaps at this stage I need to acknowledge (as Said does in relation to his own work, *Orientalism*) my personal investment in this study. As an Asian Australian (I am originally from Sri Lanka) exploration of these texts has had more than an academic interest for me.

The concept of Asia itself should be in no danger of homogenisation. In any case these texts themselves—despite the commonalities this paper will identify—assert their own vigorous heterogeneity. As critics have pointed out in these works where multi-cultural writers have chosen to explore themes of migration there is frequently a strong element of autobiography. From India, the writing of Mena Abdullah is stamped with Punjabi cultural motifs, while Christopher Cyrill's Anglo-Indian background is equally unmistakable. Yasmine Gooneratne is a Sinhalese from Sri Lanka while Brian Castro is of Chinese origin. Despite the general adherence to standard English structures in narration, the varied 'englishes' of the dialogue, the untranslated words usually referring to foods, cultural practice, literary and religious texts from these varied cultures, even the names of persons and places help refract a rich diversity.

A common motif in the selected texts is that the first-person narrator (and there is more than one within a single text) or the foregrounded consciousness is, frequently Australia-born, yet continues to retain a strong tie with and position within an Asian family. With the Australian birthright comes a hybridity of perception, an acquisition of an Austral-Asian gaze. So the child, Nimmi in the Abdullah text sees the lascar visitor as 'a dark face in a white country' (*TP*, 13). She registers her own father's speech as 'the queer English that always makes the nurse lady laugh' (*TP*, 8) In the Cyrill text the blue-eyed dark-faced boy reacts against the accents of his newly-arrived relatives:

> My uncle and aunt spoke with accents that reminded me of the accents of the men who sat on our nature strip and my father was also talking with an accent (*GT*, 28).

While the rest of the family barracks for India during a Test Match, he 'silently cheered as the Indian batsmen collapsed.' Sri Lanka-born Bharat and Navaranjini metamorphosize on-stage into Australians Barry and Jean—a process attended with much comedy and some trauma. The last word is given their Australia-born daughter, poised at the end of the novel to visit her parents' homeland on a fact-finding thesis project. Australia is the 'home' to which she will return. Seamus, in the Castro work, begins his narrative with

> Seamus O'Young. It's not my real name. I'm not Irish. I am in fact an ABC an Australia-born Chinese. (*BP*, 10)

His blue eyes have made him realise quite early that he is not 'completely Chinese.' His friend, asked to describe him, sees only the stereotype:

> You have a moonface . . . black hair sticking out of the top and your eyes are slits. Your nose is flat and you have yellow skin. . . (*BP*, 10).

He does not see those tell-tale blue eyes. Shan, the earlier Chinese visitor, also projects the sense of a hybridised vision. He describes the arrival of his group as it could have appeared to watching Australians. 'All those moonfaced men with pig-tails stepping ashore from another age' (*BP*, 73) or again 'this rag-tag army of blue-shirted moonfaced Celestials' (*BP*, 77).

Where the distanced gaze of the colonialist observer in the Conrad text can only construct the African as barely human, the gaze of the Australasian resident within a familiar environment, moves beyond a simply reductive stereotype of 'otherness.' The antagonistic Ugly Australian is encountered and contained. The Australian is also constructed as friend, as teacher (inducting the Asian into the Australian way of life), as lover, as surrogate parent, as family. Two texts, *A Change of Skies* and *Birds of Passage* straddle different historical moments and comprehend a range of perspectives on the Australian 'other.' Grandfather Edward (in the first) a nineteenth century Asian visitor arriving with a group of indentured labourers is greeted on arrival in Melbourne by a barrage of stones. In spite of this, he is still able to write at the end of his sojourn: ". . . I have met with good fortune and great kindness in many places and especially from my friend Joe. Despite the differences in our background and education . . ." (*CS*, 166). The shock of the encounter with the Anti-Asian graffitti for Edward's descendants on their arrival in Sydney is quickly erased by the kindliness of their

Australian neighbours. These neighbours, come the end of the story, become the adoptive parents of their daughter.

In Castro's novel, Seamus runs the whole gamut of rejection and violence so characteristic of early Chinese experience in Australia, yet is able to envisage a less troubled future: 'I see my descendent discovering transient moments of joy and laughter' (*BP*, 136). In the Castro novel the schoolboys' racist taunts of Shan's descendent Sheamus need to be juxtaposed with his relationship to his foster parents—particularly the woman Eddie to whom he returns in later years. She 'teaches him all she knows' and is a catalyst in his re-discovery of his Chinese heritage. The supportive role of women in the bleak Castro text could suggest the mutual empathy of the marginalised but it is a role also allocated male figures in other texts. Besides the family figure—father, mother, grandmother who induct the children into their mixed Hindu/Muslim cultural inheritance must be set such a figure as the singing Irishman who entrances the children with his own stories and songs of their adoptive culture.

Most interestingly, in Christopher Cyrill's work, it is the white Australian figures who appear as marginalised. The canvas is filled with his ebullient relations arriving in a never-ending stream from India. His white girlfriend Sussannah articulates her feelings of being excluded and at the end returns to England. His friend Jack displaced from his own home by his mother's re-marriage to a migrant, appears to lead an uneasy existence on the fringes of society. Yet he functions also as the Australian helper/teacher who inducts Christopher into the seamier aspects of life in a big city. Christopher's family's solidarity is expressed through their manner of travelling on holiday—in a convoy of eight cars, or the mass family attendance at cricket matches, and even moving house. Driving to Tullamarine airport, Christopher knows there are relatives of his in every suburb in Melbourne.

Amongst the celebratory motifs that circulate in these texts are those of births and marriages. A new baby sister is born into Nimmi's family. The young cousin's marriage to the Australian woman which sparks off a family rift is later healed by the birth of a child, who, it is acknowledged will 'belong to both worlds' (74). In the bleak narrative of Shan's life, the loyalty of a woman and the promise of new life exorcises some of the hatred and failure of his Australian experience. As Seamus' narrative also disintegrates with the onset of mental illness, there are again regenerative suggestions in the loyalty of women. In Gooneratne's cast of characters the Koyakos who remain determined to marry their daughter to a Sri Lankan—are appropriately returned to the island. The attitude articulated by Christopher's father could well serve as a comment on the significance of these recurrent motifs:

> I once wanted you to marry an Indian girl, but now I want you to mix your genes. You are an Anglo-Indian born in Australia. You are like a Trinity. Marry mix. . . . One day soon there will be only one race. . . . Drift, you must mix. Simone married a Pakistani; her children, your godson, they are everything, all, they cannot hate without hating themselves. (*GT*, 146)

Food and the ritual of eating together as a signifier of bonding requires no specialist argumentation. The cannibalism of the blacks in the Conrad narrative confers on them an extremity of savage 'otherness.' The specially prepared food of a group is emblematic of its cultural uniqueness. For the migrant it remains the tangible tie with the lost homeland. In *The Time of the Peacock*, the preparation of condiments for cooking has the air of family celebration. Not only the occasional Indian visitor, but the Irish priest Fr. Harrigan and the reclusive Paddy McCarthy share a meal with the family. The 'Australianised' grandchildren (who are also Muslim) are doubtful about their Hindu grandmother's visit and a possible meatless diet but as they grow to love her, realize

> We loved her food too. The dhal she cooked was wonderful, full of spices and strange tastes. She made curries from eggs and from all sorts of vegetables that we had never thought were vegetables at all. . . (*TP*, 36).

The trajectory of Jean's progress in the Gooneratne text is significant. An indulged young woman from an upper middle-class home, she has hardly cooked in Sri Lanka. In Sydney where the cooking of Sri Lankan food is a mode of cultural affirmation, her repertoire develops apace. When Barry evolves a project for the teaching of English to Asian students as a means of assisting their acclimatisation to Australia, Jean devises a project for a recipe book, entitled *Something Rich and Strange,* "a wholesome synthesis of East and West" (*CS*, 293) is what the book is about. Its highlight is a 'Lemon Coconut Surprise' which combines the cream of Sri Lankan coconuts with the tangy tartness of luscious Aussie citrus (*CS*, 294).[12] Christopher Cyrill's account of the numerous family gatherings is redolent with the smells, tastes and preparation of savoury dishes: tandoori chicken, parathas, Indian sweets, barfi, gulab jamun. The boy is initiated by his father into his special recipes. Australian friends like Jack and Sussannah share casually in family meals even as Indian visitors are always offered the ritual plate of rice.

A significant contrast in the Castro work is that the sense of community seems restricted to the group of Chinese in Shan's narrative. They are represented frequently sharing their austere meal of boiled rice and vegetables. It is only in the later story of Seamus that the Chinese figure is admitted into the circle of community represented by the shared meal. Then he is shown with his foster parents "a family of three" at dinner (*BP*, 38). At first his foster mother keeps on boiling rice for him till she learns 'he preferred pies, steak and chips' (*BP*, 14). Yet he deliberately eats a frog as an experiment in the laboratory at school as a mode perhaps of reaching back into his Chinese past. What this sharing of food signifies is articulated by the child Joti in the Abdullah story where the little girl has been taunted at school because of the kebabs she brings for lunch. When her new friend finds the food "tastes nice" (*TP*, 100), Joti remembering her grandfather's words about sharing is glad: ". . . we have shared our food," she shouted, "we are sisters, sisters" (*TP*, 100).

The positioning of the observer, the narratorial voice, circulating images are all key elements in the construction of a discourse of otherness, as indeed of its exorcism. How does the image of the environing landscape work? To Marlow— from his distanced position on the boat, the African landscape appears mysterious, almost a mirage; its sounds are indecipherable, totally alien. In these works, an imaginative sleight of hand superimposes the landscape of the original home onto the Australian landscape. In the Abdullah text an Indian garden redolent with the perfume of kashmiri roses and jasmine blooms on an Australian farm. Here the white peacock spreads his tail on a moonlit night as though to underline the recognition that 'here' is home. In the Gooneratne text the young woman writes home delightedly.

> Wherever I looked . . . I saw plants I have known all my life . . . a frangipani tree . . . with white and gold flowers . . . a white jasmine creeper. . . (*CS*, 171).

She encounters a 'mynah' a little bird which she believes could have come out on her grandfather's ship (*CS*, 172). Sri Lankan herbs grow in Australian gardens, planted by earlier sojourners in the land. The grandfather Edward on his earlier visit finds the beaches remind him of those beside his ancestral home. He encounters a town called 'Badagini' named after an incident centering on Sri Lankan migrants of an earlier time.

Cyrill's title *The Ganges and its Tributaries* suggests the overflowing of the Indian confluence into other landmarks. The map of India marked with family landscapes which his father floats in the pool is a symbolic gesture of the conflation of 'here' with home. The Australia-born boy dreams of places in India made known to him by his parents' stories. Frequently in his thoughts and daydreams the landscapes are interchangeable: 'here' and 'there' are both home.

> It occurred to me one day as I watched the model . . . that India had roughly the same outline as Australia. When the model turned in the water so that Nagercoil pointed directly east, I could transplant the Great Australian Bight onto the Gulf of Cambay and transplant Arnhem Land onto Calcutta (*GT*, 21).

or again he

> . . . imagined transplanting the borders, mountain ranges and seas of all the maps I could remember over the glass-scaled map of Victoria. I could then detour a traveller from St Kilda through Taxila to Dandenong, or through Lumbini to Oakleigh (*GT*, 76).

In the Castro text Shan's first reaction to Australia is that he "was anxious to be physically a part of this country" (*BP*, 62). Later in flight he shows a capacity for survival in the bush that parallels an Aborigine's skill. There is in some of these texts a persisting sense of an affinity with the Aboriginal Australian.[13] It is believed that Shan had lived amongst Aborigines during this time. Seamus, the later descendent of Shan, seems also possessed of the bush skills that have helped his ancestor at an earlier time. When he returns to the place in which he grew up despite its unfamiliarity the landscape affects him powerfully:

> As I run over the dead pine needles and feel the cones scrunch under my soles I am aware of another path, a deeper one embedded in the soil. Something seems to form the beginning of a whole history here, and I am somewhere along it. (*BP*, 47)

Entering a train compartment, Shan encounters an Aboriginal woman and reflects on the link between them: 'The native and the foreigner: there was something of both in us' (*BP*, 59).[13]

The very act of writing these texts constitutes an act of interrogation of the Orientalist discourse that up to now has 'spoken for' the Orient. They represent the acquisition of a voice which must inevitably diminish the alienness of the 'other.' In the Conrad text the blacks utter only guttural incomprehensible sounds which construct the African as more animal than human. In the Gooneratne novel the nineteenth-century white Australians are startled by the arrival of Grandfather Edward and his group of English-speaking Asians. Obviously they could not therefore be so easily relegated to the sub-human status reserved for non-whites. The fact that Edward's grandson arrives in Australia as a Professor of Linguistics ensures a less traumatic process of assimilation. His wife uses her acquired Australian idiom to vanquish the racist professor in a scene of hilarious comedy.

In the Abdullah text many of the older characters—the father, the uncle are shown to have a command of English, even if accent or phrasing provoke some mirth. While the narrative mode of these writers generally adheres to standard English structures they endeavour to reproduce the varieties of 'englishes' spoken by these characters from so many varied cultural backgrounds. Abdullah devises a stylised mode that reflects the charm and dignity of the Hindu grandmother's speech and manner. In one episode where the grandmother mourns her isolation: "Pubjabi voices," she said. "Punjabi faces. There is nothing of my people in my children here." Her granddaughter, in an attempt to please her, recalls the word 'Mirbani':

> There is no word in Punjabi like it, and there is none in English unless it is grace, the state of grace, or graciousness. . ..
>
> "What child? What?"
>
> "That is you Nani," I said, "Mirbani."
>
> Grandmother began to laugh. "I was wrong," she said, "There is the soul of the Brahmin in thee. Thou knowest how to flatter and to please. Thou knowest the words that should be true." She held me to her and talked to me, or to herself, or to God. . . (*TP*, 39).

Christopher Cyrill's characters are represented as speaking their distinctive form of English: an Indian English which in its carefree abrogation of the rules of standard English emphasises their total self-confidence.

> 'Uncle Boney,' my Aunt Kathy said, is still strong like a bull. Every month he used to 'train' it down to Banaras and sit on the ghats waiting to die. Now he's given up on death, just sits and drinks thandai from his dirty brown cup. Or sometimes he listens to some band or receives blessings from a panda. He's all hunched over now, not like when he used to wrestle and box. Still like a mandarin to all his friends.'

> 'Better he doesn't come,' my father said. 'This is a terrible country to grow old in.' (*GT*, 29)

In the Castro works the ancestor Shan has written his story in Chinese. It requires Sheamus' mediation of that narrative through his own English text to give voice to those experiences of the past. Shan has himself studied English. It confers on him a special status. As he puts it: 'I earned the privileges of being the spokesman for my people' (*BP*, 40). When he addresses Mary (the woman who is moved to follow him later), the fact that he spoke "perfect English" (*BP*, 119) reduces her initial perception of his 'otherness,' "A Chinaman . . . his pigtail over his shoulder" (*BP*, 119). Later, his retreat behind his uncomprehending "Chinaman's voice," (*BP*, 117) represents the deliberate positioning of a barrier between himself and the man Clancy, frustrating thereby the latter's wish for communication and 'brotherhood.'

Without homogenising the effects of these texts or ignoring the specificities of their varied cultural backgrounds to identify some of the commonalities they refract. In his 'Introduction' to *Orientalism* Said expressed the hope that a "better understanding of the way cultural domination has operated" could stimulate 'a new kind of dealing with the Orient': indeed it could 'eliminate 'the Orient' and 'Occident' altogether. Exploration of these texts on such lines as has been attempted here suggest that this task of deconstruction has already begun.

NOTES

1. Edward W Said. *Orientalism* (Victoria: Penguin, 1991), p. 20. First published Routledge & Kegan Paul, 1978.
2. See Flemming Brahms, 'Entering Our Own Ignorance: Subject- Object Relations in Commonwealth Literature,' *World Literature Written in English*, Vol. 21, No. 2 (Summer, 1982), pp. 233-34.
3. Chinua Achebe's rejection of this work as 'racist' and 'offensive' hardly requires argument. He saw it as a work stemming from the desire "in Western psychology to set Africa up as a foil to Europe, a place of negations . . . in comparison with which Europe's own state of spiritual grace will be manifest." *Massachussets Review*, Vol. 18, No 4, 1977, p. 783.
4. Said, p. 207.
5. Quoted in Richard White, *Inventing Australia—Images and Identity 1688-1980* (St Leonards: Allen & Unwin, 1992), p. 81.
6. Alison Broinowski, *The Yellow Lady—Australian Impressions of Asia* (Melbourne: Oxford University Press, 1992), p. 9.
7. See Abdul Jan Mohammed, 'The Economy of Manichaen Allegory,' *Critical*

Inquiry, 12 (Autumn 1985), pp. 59-87.

8. See Stephen Slemon, 'Unsettling the Empire: Resistance Theory for the Second World,' *World Literature Written in English*, Vol. 30, No 2, 1990, pp. 30-41.
9. See Sketch 'Circular Quay in the Nineties,' in Norman Lindsay, Bohemians of the Bulletin (Sydney: Angus & Robertson, 1965), pp. 8-9.
10. See Robert Drewe, *A Cry in the Jungle Bar* (Sydney, 1979); Christopher Koch, *The Year of Living Dangerously* (Melbourne, 1978); Blanche D'-Alpuget, *Turtle Beach* (Melbourne, 1981).
11. See Kateryna Arthur and Sneja Gunew, ed., *Striking Chords* (North Sydney: Allen & Unwin, 1991).
12. The author has kindly made the original recipe available to this writer.
13. There is much more to explore in this connection in all of these works. The Gooneratne text for instance, explicitly recalls shared origins in Asia.

    There must lie behind the eyes of nearly every person one sees in an Australian street the shadow of some earlier voyage. . . . For only one group among us there was no voyage. . . . Maybe they merely sauntered from one life to another . . . woke with the dawn light in one continent and pitched camp at dusk in another. . . . Maybe they are still dreaming of the Asia they left behind. . . (*CS*, pp. 151-52).

NB: Page references in the text are to the following editions:

1. Abdullah, Mena and Ray Matthew. *The Time of the Peacock.* 1965; Sydney: Angus & Robertson, 1973 Abbrev. *TP*.
2. Castro, Brian. *Birds of Passage*. Victoria: Allen & Unwin, 1993. Abbrev. *BP*.
3. Cyrill, Christopher. *The Ganges and its Tributaries*. Victoria: McPhee Gribble, 1993. Abbrev. *GT*.
4. Gooneratne, Yasmine. *A Change of Skies*. Sydney: Picador, 1991. Abbrev. *CS*.

11

"...the Novelist Skipped Town ..." A Post-script to the ICASEL Conference—Mysore[1]

Recently, Anthony Spaeth, interviewing R.K. Narayan for *Time* magazine recorded that:

> Last January a group descended on Mysore to discuss the 'Malgudization of Reality', Brahminness, and inevitably the role of women. The novelist skipped town to avoid them.[2]

Even if Mr Narayan did skip town deliberately, it only showed his own awareness (as did the *Time* account and the Conference itself) that despite the widely proclaimed 'death of the author', the literary world continues to be 'obsessively author-centred.[3] Delegates to the Conference were informed they could have the rare opportunity of meeting the novelist if they journeyed on to Madras where he spent the Indian winter months. Tight travel schedules and the exhaustion of the trip to Mysore dissuaded many. To me it offered an opportunity to check some impressions gathered from the tales with the teller himself. So I took the midnight train to Madras.[4] In Madras negotiations were concluded through a generous young woman, the novelist's grand-daughter whose concessions to my tightly-scheduled travel plans left me gushingly grateful. Next morning my life was laid in the hands of my unflappable taxi driver who, as we whirled recklessly through the Madras traffic, assured me he 'knew exactly the address' and 'we should be there very punctually'. It is one of the lesser known conveniences of travelling in India that English is so widely spoken. Whether in Mysore or Madras, Mr Narayan was widely known. My host, at the modest hotel where I'd checked in, was visibly excited that I was going to meet the great man.

The taxi driver was as good as his word. I arrived 'very punctually'. Obviously, I was expected, for with the first sound of the doorbell, the heavy security grill slid back. The door opened on what seemed, after the glare and dizzying confusion of the Madras streets, an oasis of muted colour and quiet. My taxi driver and mentor would return in two hours.

"I am Mr Narayan's nephew. My uncle is expecting you. Please be seated." This was the polite welcoming speech of the gentleman who had let me in. Mr Narayan appeared almost at once, walking with the exaggeratedly careful gait of the very old, though his carriage seemed remarkably erect. His expression appeared enigmatic, unexpectedly unsmiling and serious. Fleetingly I was disappointed, there seemed no visible sign of the genial kindness that has won him a train of faithful fans the world over. Was there a wariness, I wondered, as he greeted me, this troublesome female who had taken him up on his offer and travelled the extra distance to meet him? I registered a fleeting impression that some kind of summing up was taking place as the large eyes flickered at me through thick glasses that magnified their scrutiny even more. Clad in his cool white Indian dhoti and western-style shirt (I thought the combination symbolic), he looked his part as the Grand Old Man of Indian Writing in English.

RKN So you have come all the way from Australia. . . . Were there lots of people at the Conference?

V Yes but I don't think anyone else will be actually coming to Madras. Plane schedules are tight. As far as I know no one else planned to come. They drove round to take a look at your house in Mysore instead.

(Visible relaxation on the part of the novelist. An amused smile lit up his features.)

RKN No! Did they actually go to have a look at my house?

V Yes. Just as one goes to take a look at Anne Hathaway's cottage if one should visit Stratford-on-Avon. I suppose.

It was time, I felt, to present my credentials. I handed him a copy of my book on his work, as an opening gambit.

V I live and work in Australia but I am originally from Sri Lanka. In the foreword to this book of mine on your work I have expressed the view that perhaps it is the shared background that first drew me to study your work.

The atmosphere now was completely relaxed. The magnified eyes look up from his scrutiny of the book. I noted that he had turned immediately to the bibliography. This time a puckish grin erupted as he asked:

RKN Do you mean to say all these people have written about my work?

V Many more by now no doubt. You can see that study was completed a while ago.

RKN Yes. You haven't written about *The World of Nagaraj* or *The Talkative Man*. *A Tiger for Malgudi* is not mentioned.

V Obviously my book needs updating. In fact it is one of the reasons I'm here and why I came to the Conference. May I ask you some questions about the women in your novels?

RKN Yes of course. Let's get the work done first and then we can chat.

Narayan's novelistic career has spanned over fifty five years, a period that comprises some of the most eventful decades in Indian history.[5] The novels provide a subtle reflection of the changing social and historical context, though Narayan himself has never acknowledged any overt preoccupation with such issues. Exploration of some of the changing roles of the female figures of the novels show that they can function as a kind of barometer of changes in the larger Indian context, so I began:

V Mr Narayan, your writing spans a very long period of Indian history, from the 1930s to the 90s. It is quite possible to trace in them a kind of evolution of women's roles in India.

RKN I don't know about this. This is what academics have to do I suppose. My only concern is that the women, like all the characters must fit the pattern of my novel. Do you know what I wrote about in my letter to Professor Gowda?

V Yes he read it out to the participants at the Conference. You warned the academics not to try to analyze the novels too much. Yes, as you say, this is the way of academics. I shall only discuss some very general impressions. If the artist is regarded as being amongst the more sensitive spirits of his age his works will often encapsulate various aspect of it, perhaps, even without his conscious desire to do so.

RKN Again I can only say if you see these things in the novels, they must be there for you. For me it is the whole pattern of the novel that I care about.

From the beginning, Narayan's work registers most sensitively the situation of women uniformly subjected to the seemingly unyielding pressures of a patriarchal society. Savitri's bitter reflections are the classic examples of the feminine dilemma; "I don't possess anything in the world. What possessions can a woman call her own except her body? Everything else she has is her father's, her husband's or her sons. . ." (*DR*, 42). Shanta Krishnaswamy concludes that the position of woman in India offers a parallel to that of the Chinese woman (as analyzed by Mao Tse-tung) who carries on her back not simply the three mountains carried by Chinese man, of colonial oppression, feudal oppression and his own backwardness but the additional one of Chinese man himself: "The woman in India too has to shake off the four mountains on her back. The novel in India constitutes a rare region of enlightened lucidity where the Indian woman picks up enough courage to raise her head and ask a few awkward but pertinent questions."[6]

From the shadowy, shy retiring figures of the traditional Indian wife and mother in *Swami & Friends* (1935) and *The Dark Room* (1938) to the successful career-woman Rosie (*The Guide*, 1958) and the intrepid apostle of birth control, Daisy (*The Painter of Signs*, 1977), Narayan's novels have bodied forth the changing images of women in the Indian scene in all their fascinating variety. Yet the strain of personal conservatism was perhaps what registered most strongly in this interview.

V You must be aware of the current interest in feminist studies in literature and of course the whole movement of feminism.

RKN I hate that word. I dislike all labels. For me, people come first.

V Isn't it part of traditional Hindu teaching that the position of woman is naturally inferior to that of man? Don't the laws of Manu indicate that a woman's condition is like that of the lowest caste, the Sudras? In her lifetime a woman must be subject first to her father, then to her husband and when he is dead, to her sons.

RKN It is very wrong to think of woman as inferior. Woman is the feminine manifestation of God. She is given the name of Shakthi which means strength. The roles of mother and grandmother have always been very important in Indian culture.

V Yes but in *The Dark Room* (1941) in Savitri you show a woman who is completely powerless against the neglect and mistreatment of her husband. She makes a gesture of defiance in leaving her house, but returns in a few days simply because she has no means of maintaining her independence. Wouldn't this be particularly reflective of the plight of woman in the India at the time, the 20s and 30s?

RKN Not really, she suffers only because she has a bullying husband.

It can still happen today if a woman has a bullying husband.

In a later novel *The Guide* (1958) he does show that a woman's reaction to "a bullying husband" can take a very different path in contemporary India. Contrasted with Savitri's (and the difference in the women's names is significant) Rosie's is no quickly aborted temporary revolt, but a defiant and lasting assertion of independence. Not only does she affirm herself against the neglect of Marco, her first husband, she can even survive the exploitation of the second.

In fact in *The Dark Room*—the 'new woman' had already appeared in the person of Shanta Bai, the young woman lawyer whose attractions had led Savitri's husband into transgressions. At this stage she is only a peripheral figure and the role accorded her could imply the novelist's wariness of the type. In Bharati in *Waiting for the Mahatma* (1964) the new woman acquires a different aura.

V Would it be right to say that it is in your novel *Waiting for the Mahatma* that the liberated woman appears for the first time at the centre of the novel?

RKN When I hear that word 'liberated,' I always want to ask liberated from what?

V Well Bharati is the first female who seems to have full control over her own life. Unlike the other women in your earlier works she does not seem restricted to the traditional roles of grandmother, mother, wife. She can, it seems, even take a role in public events.

RKN Yes, this happened in Gandhi's time. Many women took part in the political movement. They saw this as their duty. The name Bharati means India.

With his use of that last word 'duty', I realised again that while the optimistic researcher could claim Bharati's activities, whether within the precincts of the Gandhian camp or fearlessly tramping lonely mountain roads with instructions from the leader, as evidence of the dawn of a revolutionary new day for the Indian female, her creator saw her as still no less firmly shackled by considerations of duty. Yet whether consciously acknowledged or not the novel refracts the cataclysmic events which had (no doubt along with a whole complex of other influences) encouraged the Indian woman to abandon her traditionally passive role. From confining herself meekly to fanning only the embers of her domestic cooking flame or tending the light before the shrine of her gods, she had stepped out to assist in kindling the flames of national revolution. For the first time the male protagonist Sriram looks on a female figure and admits, "He was frightened of her. She seemed to be too magnificent to be his wife" (*WM*, 167).

So the novels have proceeded to record these vital changes in the Indian scene. *The Guide* explored as never before the new opportunities opening before women. Rosie the temple dancer is also the holder of a degree in Economics and can marry the archaeologist Marco. Thus it seems she escapes the taboos of caste, but Marco, hoping for a compliant wife, is soon disabused. Rosie is not content to spend her days simply waiting for the whims of a man whose only concern is for his own career while forbidding her the pursuit of her own. Despite the still-lingering shackles of caste and tradition, Rosie defies all the traditional proprieties in abandoning her husband for a lover. Subsequently, this lover functions as an agent who launches her into her professional career as a dancer. When this lover falls a prey to his own acquisitiveness and goes to prison, Rosie's own talent and energy appears more than adequate to sustain her continued success.

Where Shanta Bai, the 'new woman' of *The Dark Room* is cast in the questionable role of the 'other woman', with all the negative judgement this implies, Rosie is insulated from the novelist's irony which plays so tirelessly on the central male figure of the novel. This is despite the fact that Raju's moral deterioration seems tied largely to his abandonment of tradition, his absorption into the rat-race of the modern capitalist influences which now hold full sway in Narayan's once-idyllic Malgudi. Rosie, who herself represents so much of the interplay of these forces of change is allowed to pronounce judgement on Raju: "I felt all along you were not doing right things." (*G*, 218). The once dominant male is reduced in this novel to the position of hanger-on: "she never spoke to me except as a tramp she had salvaged . . . she went through her act of help in a cold businesslike manner." (*G*, 216)

Interestingly although she seems well-equipped for a career in the modern world through her degree in Economics, Rosie achieves her independence through her dedication to her traditional occupation of dancing. The temple dancer however is transformed into a super star with erstwhile lover acting as agent and entrepreneur.

V Did you explore in Rosie some of the implications of a woman seeking self-fulfilment outside of the traditionally ordained roles?

RKN My main focus was on Raju. I simply fitted Rosie into the pattern around Raju.

In *The Sweet Vendor* (1967), Jagan—the traditional minded patriarch at the heart of the novel, gives up the struggle with the currents of change in a world he can no longer make sense of and retires to the forest. Those unnerving changes are represented mostly by the activities of the son Mali, newly-returned from America. The final shock for Jagan is the discovery that the American Chinese woman he has supposed is his son's wife, is not in fact married to him. Change in the shape of a foreign woman who lives by codes he cannot begin even to grasp has invaded the inner sanctum of Jagan's home. Here, as in others of the later works like *The Guide* the traditionally-oriented elder can only, it seems, take flight before the forces of the modern world. Rosie, Grace, Daisy are all portrayed as literally putting the traditional keepers of the Indian home to flight. Most significantly, when Raman's old aunt leaves for Benares, the images of the gods she has worshipped are taken from their place in the shrine room (to be made into Daisy's office) and put away in a drawer.

V Grace is the only Western woman who appears in your works. Western influences are so much part of the Indian scene, that I thought this unusual.

RKN It is not unusual really. I prefer to write about what I know. I don't really know Western women.

In *The Painter of Signs*, developments are revolutionary. The old aunt's words to Raman, encapsulates the reaction of the orthodox tradition-oriented Indian to Daisy's role as propagandist for population control: "She has told me all about her duties. Isn't it by God's will that children are born?" (*PS*, 54) In placing such a woman as Daisy and her birth control campaign at the centre of this novel Narayan appears to acknowledge that the movement for women's freedom has reached a kind of apotheosis on the Indian scene.

The sincerity of Daisy's commitment, the austere regimen to which she subjects herself in her tireless apostleship is projected in some detail and recalls Bharati (*Waiting for the Mahatma*). Yet Daisy's conduct represents the complete subversion of all the patriarchal codes that regulate the traditional Indian woman's life. She describes how she successfully resisted her parents' attempts at matchmaking, turning the conventional 'inspection' of the prospective bride into an inspection and rejection of the bridegroom:

> When the moment came for me to pace before the visitors coyly and reverently I just strode up like a soldier, the jewellery jingling

> and the horrible lace sari rustling, . . . and stood before the fellow. . . . They all looked a little shaken at the very style of my walk (*PS*, 133).

She ignores her mother's admonition to prostrate herself before the visitors and proceeds to interrogate the groom by turning back his own questions, "What class are you studying in?" and "Can you sing?" The situation is reduced to farce:

> It could not go on like this. Plainly the whole proposal had collapsed. A hundred eyes scowled at me. I thought they'd strangle me. But they left me alone (*PS*, 133)

The last sentence is significant. Daisy, it seems has won control over her life. When she chooses to consider marriage it is she who decrees the terms to her prospective groom. "It was Gandharva style marriage, as easily snapped as made" (*PS*, 169). She was not going to take his name, there were to be no children. "if by mischance, one was born she would give the child away and, keep herself free to pursue social work." (158) As she explains to Raman:

> Long ago I broke away from the routine of a woman's life. There are millions of women who go through it happily but I am not one of them. I have a well-defined purpose from which I will not swerve. If you want to marry me you must leave me to my own plans even when I am a wife. On any day you question why or how, I will leave you. . . (*PS*, 159).

In Daisy the Indian woman has indeed reached the apotheosis of her liberation. Later, despite all the concessions extracted from her lover, she decides the marriage will not take place. At the end Daisy leaves Raman, explaining only, "Married life is not for me, I have thought it over. It frightens me. . . . I can't live except alone" (179).

With Daisy, it would seem that Woman's Lib has come to stay in India no less than in the West. Yet more than with any other female figure in the novels, Daisy, is subjected to the full play of the author's ironic humour. Often it is registered through the disgruntled reflections of her would-be lover: "What a lot of policing she was doing! Raman thought she must really be mad! She will fight and shun people who bring up large families, some madness must have got into her head . . ." (67), or again "Was she going to force her way into every bedroom and shoo the partners apart?" (176) There is one remarkable episode where

Daisy is obliged to spend the night in a tree to escape possible rape by the impatient Raman.

V You really have a lot of fun at Daisy's expense don't you? Is this a way of showing your disapproval of the liberated woman?

RKN No, not really, I see her as a comic figure. Comic, because she is fanatical. Anyone who acts fanatically becomes laughable.

Despite the note of comedy that surrounds her, Daisy's progress shows the revolutionary changes that have taken place in the Indian scene. The sacrosanct patriarchal structures have been radically undermined. The subordination of the female to male expectations enshrouded particularly in social conventions governing marriage is no longer fore-ordained.

Undoubtedly the names he gives these women Rosie, Daisy, Grace are significant in their western derivation, names which must immediately strike the knowledgeable hearer that the woman who bears it must be caste-less, an outcast from the traditional world and its values. Yet in home after home he shows the upholder of traditional ways literally abandon their stronghold before the interloper as mother, grandmother or aunt retires vanquished before the youthful revolutionaries.

In his latest novels, *The Talkative Man* (1986) and *The World of Nagaraj* (1990), the women seem to have retired again to the background and to their traditional roles, patiently waiting on husbands and sons. Yet in the first novel, the virago who takes up residence at the local station waiting room, intending the recapture of her runaway husband there is more evidence that the Indian world has in a sense come full circle since the experience of Savitri in *The Dark Room.* Here, it is not the gentle dutiful wife fleeing from a callous philandering husband, rather the full-blooded male is in full flight from his dominating spouse, who will not tolerate his roving eye. That spouse is pictured as follows:

> a six-foot woman (as it seemed at first sight) dark-complexioned, cropped head and in jeans and a T-shirt with bulging breasts, the first of her kind in the Malgudi area . . . (*TM*, 39)

Her card, which she leaves with the Talkative Man reads "Commandant Sarasa, Home Guards Auxiliary, Delhi' (*TM*, 98). Despite her pursuit of her husband, the calls of her profession supersede love. Later she explains his second flight thus: "I could not give him enough time . . . being mostly out on official duties" (*TM*, 117). Her context is significant, the railway is only a symbol of the whole complex of social, political and economic factors that particularly in the fifty or sixty years of Narayan's writing have radically altered the Indian scene.

Yet finally it seems the extent of those changes should not be exaggerated. What the later novels illustrate, and the interview with the writer establishes is the need to preserve an awareness of the range of possibilities that still exist. I attempted to summarize some factors that seemed to emerge.

V Would you agree that in modern India women have far more opportunities for self fulfilment than ever before?

RKN Some women are happy to be in their homes looking after their families. For them it is their fulfilment.

V What about your own daughter?

RKN She is in there. (Gesturing towards an inner room) Today is a busy day. A cleaning woman comes in and she is busy going from room to room with a mop.

V Did she ever pursue a career?

RKN She is very busy and happy in what she is doing. My granddaughter is very different. She helps me with my bookshop and my business affairs.

I had in fact, spoken to this extremely pleasant and efficient young woman on the phone the night before arranging the details of my visit. Very obviously she was empowered to liaise on her grandfather's behalf. Before I left I asked whether his daughter would pose for a photograph with him. It appeared she disliked being photographed but in obvious deference to paternal insistence, acquiesced. "It will only take a minute. This lady has come all the way from Australia," he said in English. The camera clicked hastily and perhaps a trifle guiltily.

The novelist's own family it would seem provided a microcosm of the larger Indian situation, the modern woman co-exists with the traditional. Women's choices may still conform to traditional patterns but choices exist now where perhaps they did not exist before.[7]

RKN That's enough of work done. Now let us relax . . .

I was touched to realize he was concerned about an item he had noticed in that morning's newspaper which could affect my flight plans. An Air Lanka plane (he'd remembered I was returning to Colombo on an Air Lanka flight) had crash landed at Mysore airport the day before. He salvaged the paper and we checked the item, which had quite escaped my notice. No it did not appear to have been a major problem. So we talked on. I took more pictures. A copy of *A Bachelor of Arts* duly inscribed was graciously gifted to me.

On the Conference, English Literature in Mysore, diaspora:

RKN I know Professor Gowda worked very hard, over several months for the Conference.

V I think Mrs Gowda worked even harder. She had some assistants, but all the catering for all the meals was done by her.

RKN You mean Mrs Gowda provided all the meals. You see, as I told you, women are very important in the Indian set-up.

V Yes along with my Conference papers, I am taking along a recipe for Mysore peas.

RKN Did you meet Professor Narasimhaiah?

V Yes I visited his library, Conference rooms, theatre. He has excellent facilities at his Centre. I also bought a copy of his autobiography, *N for Nobody*.

RKN *N for Nobody*? (obviously amused.) He has done so much for English literature in India. His son who is also an academic will carry on his work. Did you meet many people from outside India at the Conference?

V Yes. The delegates came from the U.S., Australia, U.K., Fiji. The striking thing for me was that so many were Indians who now live abroad. Perhaps your novels recreate India for them so they feel they never left home. Ved Mehta said that for him your books have "the ring of true India."[8] Yet some of the younger ones have actually been born abroad and would know little of India anyway.

RKN I simply write about the life I know.

Other Indian writers:

RKN You cannot be reading only the novels of R.K. Narayan. Who are the other Indian writers you've read?

V Amongst the older writers, Mulk Raj Anand, Raja Rao, Bhabani Bhattacharya; the younger women writers . . . Nayantara Sahgal, Kamala Markandaya, Anita Desai, Shashi Deshpande.

RKN I enjoyed Anita Desai's *Baumgartner's Bombay*. I must say I don't have too much time to read though.

V What about the poets? Nissim Ezekiel, Dom Moraes, Kamala Das? Vikram Seth?

RKN I like Vikram Seth's work very much . . .

Australian writers:

RKN No I haven't read many. Perhaps you can send me some Australian novels. (I had enquired earlier as to what I could send him by way of a gift from Australia. I have since sent him a copy of Yasmine Gooneratne's *A Change of Skies*. It is a novel of Sri Lanka migrants in Australia, to carry on the motif of diaspora.)

V When you visited Australia some years ago, did you meet any Australian writers of interest?

RKN Yes. I remember meeting Patrick White. . . . He was a very serious man. Very polite but very serious. I think of Australia as a big, empty country. There don't seem to be people, when I compare it with this place . . . .

Critics on his work

V You said you wrote about the India you knew. How do you feel about V.S. Naipaul's criticism of your work?

RKN (with his widest grin, slowly) I don't care, **what** they say . . .

With a distinguished writing career spanning over half a century and an oeuvre which makes him a perennial contender for the Nobel Prize, R.K. Narayan can well afford to ignore the gripes of critics, no matter how eminent. For the contemporary literary world he continues to straddle the scene of Indian writing in English, a gentle, unassuming Colossus. Spaeth writes that "Lay readers want to correspond with him certain that only the nicest of men could pen the warm comedies of Malgudi." Here certainly the tales do not belie the teller, except that along with "nicest" I would add also the word "canniest". How else does his comedy also achieve that effect of astringency? Age certainly has not withered either his wit or his wisdom. One can only look forward to his next work, a collection of stories, *The Grandmother's Tale* due to be published next year.

List of Abbreviations

DR *The Dark Room*. Mysore: Indian Thought Publications, 1974. [1st publ. London: Hamish Hamilton, 1935.]

WM *Waiting for the Mahatma*. Mysore: Indian Thought Publications, 1969. [1st publ. London: Methuen, 1955.]

G *The Guide*. Mysore: Indian Thought Publications, 1970. [1st publ. New York: Viking, 1958.]
PS *The Painter of Signs*. London: Heinemann, 1977.
TM *The Talkative Man*. Ringwood, Vic.: Penguin, 1988. [1st Publ. London: Heinmann, 1986.]

NOTES

1. ICASEL—The Institute for Commonwealth and American Studies and English Language, Mysore, organised an International Conference, 'R.K. Narayan and Commonwealth Fiction in English,' 7-9 January 1992.
2. Anthony Spaeth, 'Passages from India', *Time*, Aug. 24, 1992, p. 49
3. David Lodge, *After Bakhtin, Essays on Fiction and Criticism* (London: Routledge, 1990), p. 15.
4. This involved a crazy ride to Mysore railway station defying an unusual state of curfew in Mysore. Thanks to Sudesh Mishra, Fijian Indian poet and academic, attending the Conference, I made it.
5. Narayan's last published novel is *The World of Nagaraj* (London: Heinemann, 1990). Since this interview, he has published *The Grandmother's Tale*.
6. Shantha Krishnaswamy, *The Woman in Indian Fiction in English* (New Delhi: Ashish, 1984), p. 8.
7. The author acknowledges permission granted by the Indian Ocean Review to use here a substantial section of an earlier article by her which appeared in that publication.
8. Ved Mehta, "The Train has just arrived at Malgudi Station", *The New Yorker*, Vol. XXXVIII, 15 Sept. 1962, p. 5.

Appendix

Kindling Australian Studies in Korea

The Australian Studies Institute at Chung Ang University South Korea was established in 1990 through the joint efforts of a group of academics drawn from a variety of departments at Edith Cowan University's School of Community and Language Studies and the Faculty of Education of Chung Ang University. Initially it was the brain child of Dr Hyung Shik Kim of the department of Community and Behavioural Studies (Edith Cowan University), a former graduate of Chung Ang and Dr Brian Lawrence, Dean of Edith Cowan University. The actual birth, after prolonged pre-natal pangs, was presided over by Dr Edwin Jaggard (Social Sciences), continued monitoring being taken over by Dino Gava of the same department. The post-natal trauma was still continuing when I succeeded to the position of resident Australian co-director in Seoul in the second semester of 1990.[1]

The intention to teach courses with Australian content dated from the inception of the Institute, but the actual status of the courses had not been finally worked out despite some sensitive initial negotiating. In an intimidatingly huge city like Seoul (population 12m), the plight of the non-Korean-speaking foreigner should not be underestimated and not till the agonising problem of accommodation was finally settled (and I had moved residences three times) was I able to give my full attention to the next challenge of working on Institute courses. My predecessors had put together a course incorporating socio-historical materials, and (as if mindful of James Walter's reminder) had also remembered the need 'to put politics back in'.[2]

I was responsible for shaping a basic course in Australian literature which would reflect some of the key emphases highlighted in the first course and also convey the range and variety of the Australian literary achievement. The two courses would therefore ride to some extent in tandem and would be designated 'Australian Perspectives I' and

'Australian Perspectives II', respectively. For the moment they led an uneasy existence as volunteer courses, initially attended by small groups of students whom our Korean co-director could persuade (coerce?) into attending. But the fact that we also had the opportunity to 'slot in' and teach in already established university courses for which our individual expertise fitted us (provided the appropriate department would tolerate the intrusion) enabled us to recruit a few students through our own powers of persuasion. Needless to say these proved the most permanent. This article focuses on the problems of structuring a course in Australian literature as a viable-component of a course in Australian Studies for Korean undergraduate students.

A most important development, for us, was the creation of a new department of International Relations at Chung-Ang University. Some fortunate lobbying secured the diplomatic assistance needed for what the Korean professors generally regarded as a historic development—the acceptance of our courses as courses for credit within the new department at second-year level. For the moment at least it seems as if the course will retain its present character which, as seems to be the norm with Australian Studies Programs, recognises the centrality of history and literature to the enterprise. As James Walter notes (in the article cited earlier) this trend continues despite the strong case being made for science and technology in the recent CRASTE Report. Our arrangement in Korea allows for a high degree of flexibility, for while the basic framework of the courses are set out in the course booklets, each new co-director can also freely add materials from his/her own particular area of expertise. For example, in semester two of this year, a staff member from the Music Academy will be resident co-director. Besides teaching the core literature-based 'Australian Perspectives II' unit, he already has plans in hand as to how Korean audiences will benefit from his own considerable expertise in his chosen field. Reports from the current (Semester 1) co-director, teaching 'Australian Perspectives I" indicated the course was being well received, despite early qualms about possible problems for some students whose skills in English might not have been as strong as could have been desired.

The teaching of the literature-based 'Australian Perspectives II' will be the real challenge. The course booklet which will serve as a base for the course produced with so much difficulty on a faulty computer, liable to throw tantrums and reduce our hardworking Korean secretary to a state bordering on breakdown, will be, one hopes, only a starting point from which a sensitive teacher can constantly adapt, change, even omit, according to the perceived needs of the students. In accordance with the need to keep it somehow tuned to the social sciences oriented course of the first semester, the course observes four basic phases of development, each given a title indicative of the theme. For example the early phase designated 'Settlement' deals with works in which the themes of settlement and convictism predominate. A phase designated 'Growing Nationalism' follows, focussing primarily on the work of Lawson and Paterson, the nationalists of the 1890s. Then comes a consideration of the continuance of the 'bush tradition' and the social realists of the 1930s under the caption 'Nationalism continued'. Post-war developments and the new sophistication, self-confidence and expansion of themes and techniques in the works of writers are regarded as justifying the titling of the latest segment, 'Maturity'.

Newer streams of writing, particularly from Aboriginal writers, and migrant writing were highlighted as a useful adjunct to the segments on multi-Culturalism with which the previous unit closes. Part of the problem in structuring the course was to ensure that it could also be used to service English majors if it was at some later stage agreed that it could be offered within the department of English Language and Literature. This is quite conceivable in the near future, since Korean professors of literature have evinced a warm interest in the possibility of expanding their own areas of expertise to include Australian literature. One of them, who became involved in the project for the translation of Patrick White's novel *The Tree of Man* into Korean, may be visiting Australia on a 'familiarisation tour' designed to further stimulate her interest and involvement.

If Australian literature could find itself a toehold in the University's department of English Language and Literature's offerings, the Institute's objectives would be promoted in the most significant way. Students of literature could naturally be expected to have higher language skills. Certainly, teaching some of these students in the 'normal' literature classes had led me to recognise they had a stamina for reading which Australian students do not often demonstrate!

For the students in the department of International Relations, the challenges could be many, but since the materials finally included were the result of practical experimentation with a mixed group of volunteer students, I am fairly confident it will work successfully. The keenness of Korean students to improve their English cannot be underestimated, and even if not prompted by the desire to obtain, through literature, a glimpse into the Australian soul as it were, they could be boosted by the hope that the course would at least improve their facility with the English language in general.

The inclusion of some amount of translation of the texts was a necessary strategy. (All of Shakespeare is available in Korean translation as well as several of the American classics; the usual procedure in departments of literature being to study the texts in English as well as in Korean translation). With selected novels—very few—for obvious reasons of their length, I resorted to a system of lengthy plot summary. This could be translated and often supplemented by a video. An extract from the original text which could be assumed to convey some sense of the author's style, and of the novel's 'flavour' could be discussed and studied at some length. Poetry, as always, presents real problems for the translator. My strategy was to provide a kind of paraphrase and a translation of the paraphrase so that even the weaker students would be assured of some measure of understanding. Since all Korean students study English through all the years of high school, their reading and comprehension skills tend to be much better than their spoken English would indicate.

The genre I drew on most frequently was the short story. From the 1890s to the present time, the Australian short story has provided an invaluable insight into Australian life and culture. Frank Moorhouse points out that 'It is risky to make social extrapolations from action, but fiction is rich in clues and signs' and regards his particular selection as being able 'to reflect accurately the way Australians live'.[3] It was possible to read and discuss several texts in the original and my small volunteer group remained remarkably faithful throughout the semester, developing into a friendly group of talkative enthusiasts constantly comparing their impressions of Australian life with their Korean experience.

Two factors remained paramount in my selection of materials for the courses. First, the need to convey to Korean audiences the sense of a 'new' literature, markedly different from the British tradition. Harpur's 'Midsummer Noon in an Australian Forest' and Kendall's 'The Last of his Tribe' marked useful points of departure, being poems on Australian subjects composed by poets consciously proud of their 'Australianness'.

Discussions with Korean professors as well as with students established very early that a 'new' English literature which could provide for departures from the perceived constrictions of Eurocentric biases was a substantial argument for the introduction of Australian literature into the curriculum.[4] Perhaps it was the outcome of having taught literature in so many different cultural contexts (Sri Lanka, Nigeria, Australia and now Korea) that prompted my instinctive sifting through for thematic issues which cut across cultural barriers and to underline that essential humanity, which despite the disagreements of critics, remains the special attribute of literature to underline. So, when our reading of Henry

Lawson's 'The Drover's Wife' was completed and one young Korean declared, 'This is the story of my own mother' I felt my choices had been approved. It is perhaps worth noting here that when the decision to select a Patrick White novel for translation into Korean was taken, the choice fell on *The Tree of Man.* The Korean professors making the decision felt that a book dealing on the one level with the struggles of a simple farmer could also appeal as a Korean version of Everyman.

Miles Franklin's *My Brilliant Career* evoked an unexpectedly warm response from the women students in the group. In a strongly male-oriented society, in which the woman nevertheless is the keystone of the family arch, regarded as the dominant formative influence behind every individual achievement, the winds of change have begun to blow as women's potential begins to crave for recognition outside of the home and family.[5]

Generally, the idea of a distinctive national identity gradually defining itself in defiance of the overwhelming influence of a dominant culture is one to which Koreans are particularly receptive. Korean history over hundreds of years has been shadowed by Chinese and Japanese colonialism, yet has continued to cling fiercely to its own uniqueness. I have probably over-sold the nationalist element in Australian writing, but the bias is one that can be amended once Koreans have come to recognise Australian literature as one worthy of attention.

The sense of difference had also to be harnessed as a stimulus to interest, beginning with facts and figures such as the Australian land mass and its infinitesimal population compared with South Korea's land mass (99,143 sq kms) and population (42m approx). Thanks to the generosity of the Commonwealth Department of Foreign Affairs, the Institute is endowed with an unusually well equipped library and many beautifully illustrated volumes of Australia's unique flora and fauna. These, supplemented with some excellent video materials, could provide the initial provocation to explore the new and intriguing. One young Korean showed his grasp of the differences in context, when, presented with a boomerang for being the 'most enthusiastic' student of Australian literature, he declared: 'Where, in Seoul, will I have the space in which to throw this boomerang?'

A guest lecture I gave at the Institute of British Commonwealth Studies at Seoul National University, on Australian Literature was entitled 'From Convicts and Kangaroos to the Nobel Prize'. I adopted the same initial strategy which had paid dividends with the different student groups. I began with unfolding a beautifully presented map of South-East Asia to demonstrate that of all the countries of the 'West', Australia's physical contiguity made it so obviously a close neighbour in our modern global village. Circulation of photographs of Australian diggers arriving at Kimpo Airport during the Korean War was visible evidence that Australians in the past had taken their neighbourly commitments seriously, and produced a notably animated reaction.

The continued success of the Institute's activities will relate directly for a while yet to the personalities of the constantly changing resident Australian co-directors. Each co-director establishes and extends further the circle of contacts and activities of the Institute. It will be important to ensure some degree of continuity in these activities. At this point, the Australian Studies Institute at Chung-Ang promises the hope of continuing dialogue between Australia and Korea. The recent Commonwealth Government grant of $42,000 to the Institute is a recognition of its potential.

NOTES

1. The resident Australian Co-director (in Seoul) changes every semester. A permanent head of the Institute continues at Edith Cowan University in Perth.
2. James Walter, 'Putting Politics Back In', *Australian Studies*, 12, Oct 1989, pp. 39-43.
3. Frank Moorhouse, *Introduction to The State of the Art* (Melbourne: Penguin, 1983), p. 23.
4. Doireann Macdermott makes a similar point in her discussion of Australian literary studies in Spain, 'Contexts as well as Texts', *Australian Studies*, 11, April 1989, p. 221.
5. See Choi Jin-young 'Korea's New Woman', in *One Woman's Way* (Seoul: Korea Herald, 1988), pp. 279-80.

Index